# THE GIANT

## Book of PRESCHOOL IDEAS for Children's Ministry

## Group

Loveland, Colorado
group.com

# Group resources really work!

This Group resource incorporates our R.E.A.L. approach to ministry. It reinforces a growing friendship with Jesus, encourages long-term learning, and results in life transformation, because it's

**Relational**
Learner-to-learner interaction enhances learning and builds Christian friendships.

**Experiential**
What learners experience through discussion and action sticks with them up to 9 times longer than what they simply hear or read.

**Applicable**
The aim of Christian education is to equip learners to be both hearers and doers of God's Word.

**Learner-based**
Learners understand and retain more when the learning process takes into consideration how they learn best.

# The Giant Book of Preschool Ideas for Children's Ministry

Visit our website: group.com

CREDITS
*Contributing Authors:* Jody Brolsma, Sheila Halasz, Marsha Hall, Rhonda Haslett, Amy Houts, Jan Kershner, Nancy Moore, Karen Pennington, Barbara Price, Janet Reeves, Donna Simcoe, Amy Weaver
*Chief Creative Officer:* Joani Schultz
*Executive Editor:* Christine Yount Jones
*Managing Editor:* Jennifer Hooks
*Editor:* Owen Shattuck
*Associate Editor:* Scott Firestone IV
*Copy Editor:* Becky Helzer
*Cover Illustration:* Chris Boyd
*Cover Design:* Jeff Spencer
*Senior Art Director:* Rebecca Swain
*Senior Designers:* Jean Bruns, Kate Elvin
*Interior Illustration:* Patrick Girouard/Portfolio Solutions, LLC; Andrew Hill; iStockphoto.com/misterelements

Unless otherwise indicated, all Scripture quotations are taken from the *Holy Bible* New Living Translation, copyright © 1996, 2004, 2007, 2013. Used by permission of Tyndale House Publishers, Inc., Carol Stream, Illinois 60188. All rights reserved.

ISBN 978-1-4707-1886-2

10 9 8 7 6 5 4 3 2 1    19 18 17 16 15

Printed in the United States of America.

# Contents

# Introduction

**I**s there anything more valuable in preschool ministry than a great idea? You might have the perfect facility, the most up-to-date check-in system, and an army of volunteers. (Okay, maybe that's a dream.) But what you really need are ideas that appeal to the heart of a preschooler.

Whether you're a preschool ministry veteran or just starting the adventure, this book is packed with all the ideas you need, when you need them: now! Each of the more than 175 ideas in this book is designed to help you introduce preschoolers to Jesus and the Bible—in relational, experiential, and fun ways.

## Get Set, Go!

Here's a snapshot of the different ways you can use this book to find the idea you need. **And be aware that bold text within each chapter is spoken text.**

### TOPIC

Each idea is categorized by topic. If you're looking for a specific lesson or theme topic, simply scan the topics in the Table of Contents on page 3, or see the Topic Index on page 179.

### CATEGORY

*The Giant Book of Preschool Ideas for Children's Ministry* provides numerous ways to quickly find the idea you need. You'll find comprehensive indexes beginning on page 175 arranged in categories including Action Plays, Bible Experiences, Crafts, Games, Prayers, Songs, and Snacks.

### SCRIPTURE

Many ideas have a direct Scripture link. To find an idea based on a Scripture, just go the Scripture Index on page 178.

## Safety First!

**Allergy Alerts**

ALLERGY ALERT! Be aware that some kids have allergies to certain foods and other materials. The ideas in this book that include these items have an Allergy Alert symbol. Always check with parents beforehand to see whether children have allergies or dietary concerns.

**Balloon Warning**

BALLOON WARNING! Children under 8 years of age can choke or suffocate on uninflated or broken balloons. Adult supervision required. Keep uninflated balloons away from children. Discard broken balloons at once. Balloons may contain latex.

# God Made the World and Us

## Genesis 1:1-31; 2:7-9, 18-22

## God Made It All

## Bible Experience

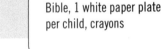

**SUPPLIES**

Bible, 1 white paper plate per child, crayons

**H**ave children sit in a circle with you. Open your Bible to Genesis 1. Show children the words, and tell them the Bible is God's special book.

Say: **The first part of the Bible tells us about how God made our wonderful world. Let's see what God made!**

Give each child a white paper plate, and set out crayons for kids to share.

**God made day and night. Choose a dark crayon and color one side of your paper plate dark, like night.** Allow time.

**Hold up your night sky for everyone to see!** Have kids wave their dark-sided plates in the air. **Now let's color the other side a bright color like the sun. Choose yellow, orange, or pink—just make it bright and sunny.** Allow time, and assist preschoolers as needed. **Now hold up your daytime sky for everyone to see.** Have kids wave their light-sided plates in the air.

**God also made land and the plants that grow on the land. Let's pretend we're little seeds that can grow into big, tall plants.** Have kids crouch down, holding their light-sided plates above their heads. Have them slowly stand, little by little, as you continue. **As the sun shines on us little seeds, we grow…and grow…and grow!**

**God also made the oceans and the fish that swim in the water. Let's pretend our plates are waves in the ocean.** Have kids hold their plates in front of them and wave their plates up and down and side to side.

**And God made birds that fly. Let's pretend our plates are birds that can fly around the room!** Have kids hold their plates in the air and pretend to fly around the room.

**Then God made animals—all *kinds* of animals! Hold your plate against your tummy and pretend you have a bear's belly. Let's hear you growl and roar!** Pause as kids pretend to be bears.

**After God made all those things, he made something even more special. He made people! Use a crayon to draw a face on the sunny side of your plate.** Pause for kids to draw. **Now hold your face plate up high, and go around the room saying hello to everyone else.** Pause as kids walk around and say hello to one another.

Ask:

- *What are some special things about you?*

Say: **God is so amazing. He made the world and us, too! Let's thank God for all he made!** Have kids stand in a circle with their plates. Go around the circle and let each child take a turn holding his or her plate in the air and saying, "Thank you, God!"

Close with a cheer for God as kids all wave their plates.

# Colorful Creations

## Craft

**SUPPLIES**

8 ½ x 11 sheets of white paper, pen, an assortment of dried-out markers, smocks (optional), paper towels, 3 or 4 clear containers with tight-fitting lids, water, tape

Give each child a piece of paper, and write the child's name on it. Before starting this activity, you may want to put a smock on each child. Say: **Let's make some paint so you can paint your favorite part of God's creation. You might paint a tree, a dog, a person, or something else.** Put several similar colors of dried-out markers in the jars with just a little water. Secure the lids, and let children take turns shaking the containers to make new colors. (The colors will intensify the longer they're allowed to develop.) Set the containers in the center of a table and give kids paintbrushes. Encourage kids to paint a favorite part of God's creation.

When kids have finished, lay the masterpieces flat to dry and then hang them up.

# What Am I?
## Game

**SUPPLIES**

1 copy for every 6 kids of the "Animals" handouts (at the end of this chapter), scissors

**Teacher TIP**

If you have a large group, let kids act out the animals in pairs.

**B**efore kids arrive, cut apart the animals on the two "Animals" handouts. You'll need one animal per child. Say: **Let's play a game to remember some of the different animals God made.**

Have kids sit in a circle. Give each child a picture of an animal to act or sound like. Then have kids each place their picture facedown on the floor and sit on it. Invite children, one at a time, to act or sound like the animal picture they were given as other kids try to guess the animal. After someone guesses the correct animal, have everyone act or make sounds like that animal. Then it'll be the next child's turn.

When the game is over, remind kids that God made all creatures. Pray: **Thank you, God, for all the different animals you made.**

# Fun Faces
## Snack

**SUPPLIES**

English muffins, soft cream cheese, raisins, strawberries, grapes, coconut, plastic knives and spoons, small paper plates, 6 paper or plastic bowls, napkins, antibacterial gel (optional)

**ALLERGY ALERT!** See page 5

**B**efore kids arrive, cut the grapes and strawberries in half, and split the English muffins into top and bottom halves. Place the remaining ingredients in separate bowls, each with a plastic spoon.

Say: **God made people. He made you** (point to a child)**, and you** (point to another child)**, and all of us! Let's make fun snacks to remind us that God made people!**

Have children clean their hands before they prepare their snacks. Then invite a willing child to pray, thanking God for making people. Provide children each with a plastic knife and a muffin half on a paper plate, and encourage kids to spread cream cheese on their muffins. Then kids can create faces on their muffin halves using the other ingredients, such as raisins for eyes, a grape half for a nose, a strawberry half for a mouth, and coconut for hair. As kids work, ask them to name people they're glad God made, adding that you're thankful God made them. When their fun face snacks are made, let kids eat and enjoy!

**SUPPLIES**

# Song

**S**ay: **Let's sing a song about God making the world and us.** Teach preschoolers the following words to the tune of "Frère Jacques."

Sing:

**God made daytime,**

**God made nighttime,**

**Shores and seas,**

**Bunnies and bees!**

**God made the world around us,**

**All the world around us,**

**You and me!**

**You and me!**

**God made doggies,**

**God made froggies,**

**Penguins and peas,**

**Flowers and trees!**

**God made the world around us,**

**All the world around us,**

**You and me!**

**You and me!**

# Thank You, God

## Action Play

SUPPLIES

**R**ead your preschoolers the following rhyme about Creation, having them follow along as you do the actions in parentheses while you read each line.

Rhyme:

**God made the sun to shine so bright,** *(make a circle above your head with your arms and hands)*

**And stars to shine all through the night.** *(put your open hands in the air and wiggle your fingers)*

**He made water and waves,** *(make wave motions with your hands)*

**And fish that swim.** *(make swimming motions with your arms)*

**And bushes and trees** *(stretch your arms up high)*

**That sway in the wind.** *(wave your arms back and forth above your head)*

**He made bears that stand up very tall,** *(stretch your arms straight overhead)*

**And little bugs that know how to crawl.** *(crouch down and wiggle your fingers)*

**He made people like us, big and small.** *(stretch your arms out to the side; then put your hands close together, palms facing each other)*

**We're thankful that God made them all.** *(cross your hands over your heart)*

# I Spy Prayer

## Prayer

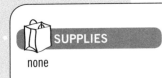

SUPPLIES

**G**ather your preschoolers in a circle on the floor. Explain that you want to thank God for making the world and us. Say that you'll start the prayer by naming something or someone God made that you're thankful for. Then go around the circle, letting each child name something or someone he or she is thankful for.

Keep going around the prayer circle until everyone's out of ideas. To help kids think of what to say, encourage them to look around the room, to look out the window, to think of their families and homes, and to think of different places they like to visit. Once they get the hang of it, it's likely your prayer will go on and on. And that's a good thing!

Close your prayer time by having kids shout out in unison, "Thank you, God!"

# Animals (1)

THE **GIANT** BOOK OF PRESCHOOL IDEAS FOR CHILDREN'S MINISTRY

# Animals (2)

# God Tells Noah to Build an Ark

## Genesis 6:11-22; 7:6–8:19; 9:8-17

## God Keeps His Promise to Noah

### Bible Experience

**SUPPLIES**

Bible, masking tape

**B**efore kids arrive, use masking tape to create a boat shape on the floor that's large enough for everyone in your group to sit inside later on.

Have children sit in a circle on the floor with you. Open your Bible to Genesis 6. Show children the words, and tell them the Bible is God's special book.

Say: **In Genesis 6, the Bible tells us about a man named Noah. God told Noah to build a big boat called an ark. God told Noah what kind of wood to use and how big the ark should be.**

**Let's pretend we're helping Noah build the ark.** Have kids imitate your motions as you tell them about Noah.

**First we'll cut some wood.** Pretend to hold a piece of wood with one hand and use a saw with the other hand.

**Now let's carry our heavy wood pieces over here to put our ark together.** Pretend to carry heavy wood over to the boat shape you taped on the floor.

**Next we need to nail all this wood together.** Pretend to hammer a nail as you build the ark on the boat shape.

**This is hard work! I'm ready for a break!** Have everyone lie on the floor and count to 10 with you. **Okay, our break's over. Time to get back to work.**

**Noah and his family finished building the ark, just as God told them to do. God said he was going to send a big flood. But God also said he'd save Noah's family plus two of every animal on the earth. That's why the ark had to be so big. It was going to hold *lots* of animals!**

Pretend to shade your eyes with your hand and look into the distance. **Look! Here come the animals! God sent two of every animal to get on the ark. Here come the lions! And here come the turtles—they're pretty slow. And look at the kangaroos jumping around. Boing! Boing!** Encourage kids to join in by naming animals as if those animals are getting on the ark and describing the actions of those animals.

Now sit with kids on the floor inside the boat shape. **The ark rocked slowly on the water.** Rock gently from side to side. **After a while, Noah noticed that the waves were getting bigger.** Rock back and forth harder. **And bigger.** Rock harder. **And bigger.** Rock harder. **Then there was a flash of lightning and a loud rumble of thunder.** Pat the floor with your hands. **The rain started.** Pat your thighs. **It rained harder and harder.** Pat more quickly. **It was a terrible storm.** Alternate between making rain and thunder sounds while still rocking back and forth.

**It rained for 40 days and 40 nights. That's a very long time.**

Ask:

- *What do you think it might've sounded like inside the ark?*
- *What do you think it might've smelled like?*

Say: **With all those animals and people, it was probably loud inside the ark. And it was probably stinky, too.** Hold your nose.

**Finally, the rained slowed down. And then it stopped. Hooray!** Have kids clap and cheer with you.

**When the ark came to rest on dry ground, Noah let out the animals. Noah and his family were glad to be outside again. It felt so good to stretch.** Lead kids in stretching.

**God sent a beautiful sign to Noah and his family to say that he would never again flood the entire earth. And that sign is for us, too! The sign is a rainbow.** Trace an imaginary rainbow over your head by waving your hands from one side of your body to the other. **Every time you see a rainbow in the sky, remember that God keeps his promises.**

THE **GIANT** BOOK OF PRESCHOOL IDEAS FOR CHILDREN'S MINISTRY

# Ark Animals

## Craft

**SUPPLIES**

white paper plates cut into halves, scissors, crayons, stapler, heavy construction paper or small sheets of poster board, 1 copy per child of the "Ark Animals" handout (at the end of this chapter)

**B**efore children arrive, cut out the animals on the "Ark Animals" handout so each child has a set of animals to color. Give children each a paper-plate half. This will be their ark. Staple the curved part of the half-plate to a sheet of heavy construction paper or poster board for each child.

Let kids color their paper-plate arks. Then let kids have fun placing their animals in and out of the ark!

# Into the Ark

## Game

**SUPPLIES**

masking tape, copies of the "Animal Cards" handout (at the end of this chapter), tape, 2-foot lengths of yarn, scissors

**B**efore kids arrive, cut apart the animals on the "Animal Cards" handout. You'll need one animal card per child. Tape the ends of a piece of yarn to the back of each card. Use masking tape to create a boat shape on the floor that's large enough for everyone in your group to sit inside. (If you used the "God Keeps His Promise to Noah" Bible experience at the beginning of this chapter, you can use the same boat shape you created for that activity.)

Choose two children to be "Noahs." Have the Noahs stand facing each other and join hands to form an arch. Give the other children each an animal card to wear around their neck. They're the animals on the ark. Have the animals line up and walk under the Noahs' arch as you repeat this rhyme:

Rhyme:

**Into the ark, two by two;**

**God sent animals, just like you!**

As the rhyme ends, have the Noahs lower their arms to catch the child walking under the arch at that moment. Send the child who was caught to the boat shape on the floor. Keep playing until all of the animals are on the ark.

When the game is over, choose two new Noahs and play again.

# Orange Arks

## Snack

**SUPPLIES**

seedless oranges or clementines cut in half, animal crackers, spoon, small paper plates, paper or foam bowls, antibacterial gel (optional)

ALLERGY ALERT!
See page 5

**B**efore kids arrive, scoop out the sections of the orange halves, keeping the peel intact, and place them in bowls. Have kids clean their hands, and give each child a plate with a scooped-out peel—this will be the ark. Then give each child a bowl with orange sections and a handful of animal crackers.

Let kids have fun placing their animals in and out of the ark for a few moments before you give thanks to God for the snack and allow kids to eat.

As kids eat, remind them that God used the ark to keep Noah's family and two of every kind of animal safe during the flood.

# Two By Two

## Song

**SUPPLIES**

**S**ay: **Let's sing a song about how God told Noah to build an ark.** Teach preschoolers the following words to the tune of "The Ants Go Marching."

Sing:

**God sent the animals two by two,**

**Hurrah, hurrah.**

**God sent the animals two by two,**

**Hurrah, hurrah.**

**He sent the animals two by two,**

**The ark became a floating zoo.**

**And they all went sailing off,**

**In the ark,**

**In the ark, two, three, four.**

**God sent the** [name an animal] **two by two,**

Hurrah, hurrah.

**God sent the** [name an animal] **two by two,**

Hurrah, hurrah.

**He sent the** [name an animal] **two by two,**

**The ark became a floating zoo.**

**And they all went sailing off,**

**In the ark,**

**In the ark, two, three, four.**

Sing the song through several times, changing animal names each time.

# Build a Boat

## Action Play

**SUPPLIES**

**R**ead your preschoolers the following rhyme about Noah, having them follow along as you do the actions in parentheses while you read the lines.

Rhyme:

**God told Noah**

**Build a boat, build a boat.** *(hammer your fists together)*

**Make sure the boat's**

**Gonna float, gonna float.** *(make wave motions with your hands)*

**I'll send animals**

**Two by two.** *(hold up two fingers on each hand)*

**To make that boat**

**A floating zoo.** *(make monkey sounds while scratching your sides like a monkey)*

**God sent rain,**

**It poured and poured.** *(make raindrops coming down with your fingers)*

**It rained for days,**

**Then it rained some more.** *(make raindrops coming down with your fingers)*

**It finally stopped,**

**And the ark hit ground.** *(crouch down and touch the ground with your hands)*

**They all came out**

**and looked around.** *(look around with your hand shielding your eyes)*

**They looked down low,**

**And they looked up high.** *(point up)*

**They saw God's rainbow**

**In the sky.** *(make an arch over your head with your arms)*

**SUPPLIES**

# Animal Thanks

## Prayer

**H**ave kids sit in a circle on the floor with you. Start the prayer by thanking God for keeping Noah and his family safe on the ark. Then thank God for keeping the animals safe on the ark. Go around the circle, and let each child name an animal he or she is thankful for. Close the prayer by thanking God for sending the rainbow as a reminder that he keeps his promises.

# Ark Animals

# Animal Cards

# God Promises Abraham and Sarah a Baby

## Genesis 18:1-16; 21:1-7

## A Beautiful Promise

### Bible Experience

 **SUPPLIES**

Bible, washcloths or dust cloths, play food, pots and pans, plates, cooking utensils

**H**ave kids sit in a circle on the floor with you. Open your Bible to Genesis 18, and show children the words. Tell them the Bible is God's special book.

Say: **The Bible tells us about a man named Abraham and his wife, Sarah. They were very old.**

Ask:

- *Who are some older neighbors or relatives you know?*

Say: **Abraham and Sarah were very old—Abraham was almost 100 years old! They had waited and waited to have a baby, but it never happened.**

**Let's see what waiting is like.** Have kids stand with their arms stretched up high. Tell them they'll have to wait until you tell them to put their arms down. Have kids keep their arms up for a minute, if possible. Kids will probably complain and want to put their arms down, but you'll want them to get the idea of waiting for something. Let them lower their arms and sit again.

**You had to wait a long time to lower your arms.**

Ask:

- *What was waiting like for you?*

Say: **Waiting can be hard. Abraham and Sarah had waited and waited to have a baby. But it just hadn't happened. At least, not yet.**

**One day, three men came to visit. Abraham hurried to greet his guests and invite them in. He asked Sarah to bake bread and make a meal for the visitors.**

**Let's pretend we're helping Abraham and Sarah prepare for guests.** Have kids pretend to clean your room for company. They can use washcloths or dust cloths to dust the tables and windowsills. They can pick up toys and stack books and blocks.

Then let kids pretend to make a meal for visitors. They can set play food on plates and use pots and pans to pretend to cook.

After a few more minutes of play, gather kids in a circle on the floor again.

Say: **When everything was ready, Abraham and Sarah gave their visitors the meal. They didn't realize that God had sent these visitors with a message—a very important message.**

**Let's practice giving a message.** Whisper "God loves you" to the child next to you, and have him or her whisper the same thing to the next child. Continue around the circle until the message returns to you.

**Abraham was sitting with the visitors outside. And Sarah was listening inside the tent. One of the visitors said: "I'll come back in about a year, and your wife, Sarah, will have a baby—a son." That was the message the three visitors came to give.**

**When Sarah heard this message, she laughed to herself because she knew she was too old to have a baby. Let's hold our bellies and laugh!** Lead kids in laughing.

**But God promised Abraham and Sarah they would have a baby. And that's just what happened. About a year later, they had a baby boy. And they named him Isaac.**

**Let's give a cheer for God because he keeps his promises.** Lead kids in clapping and shouting, "Yay, God!"

# Baby Blanket

## Craft

**SUPPLIES**

1-inch squares of colorful fabric or paper, glue sticks, crayons, 1 copy per child of the "Baby Isaac" handout (at the end of this chapter)

**D**istribute a "Baby Isaac" handout to each child. Say: **God promised Abraham and Sarah a baby. And that baby was little Isaac! Babies need to stay nice and warm. That's why in your picture baby Isaac has a blanket over him. Let's make him even warmer by adding some colorful squares to his blanket!**

Set out glue sticks, crayons, and the squares of fabric or paper. Have kids color the picture and then glue the squares on the blanket. They can take their pictures home as reminders that God keeps his promises!

# Food Folly

## Game

**SUPPLIES**

plastic loaves of bread (or other plastic food items), masking tape

**U**se tape to create two 4-foot-long parallel lines on the floor about 10 feet apart.

Say: **When God sent three visitors to Abraham and Sarah, Sarah baked bread and made food for the visitors. Since the visitors were waiting, maybe Sarah had to hurry. Let's play a hurry-up food game to remind us of the promise the three visitors came to deliver.**

Have kids form two single-file lines behind one of the tape lines. Give the first person in each line a plastic food item to hold on outstretched hands. When you say "go," those kids will speed-walk to the other tape line and back, balancing the food on their out-stretched hands.

When they get back to the first tape line, they'll hand off the food to the next child, who'll repeat the process. If a child drops the food, he or she can simply pick it up and resume the race. As kids race, have everyone else call out words of encouragement.

# Dough Dabs

## Snack

**H**ave kids clean their hands. Then give each child a small handful of thawed bread dough on a paper plate, telling them the dough is not to eat.

Say: **When God sent visitors to tell Abraham that Sarah would have a baby, Sarah baked bread to feed the visitors. Before you bake bread, the dough has to be kneaded. Let me show you what I mean.** Demonstrate how to knead a small amount of dough with your hands. Then let kids do the same with their dough.

After several minutes of kneading, set aside the dough and have children clean their hands. Then give each child a slice of bread on a paper plate. Thank God for the good food he provides; then let kids eat and enjoy!

(You can send home the dough in resealable plastic bags for families to bake, along with baking instructions from the package, or bake the dough during the lesson and send home the rolls with kids.)

# Ha Ha, Hee Hee

## Song

**S**ay: **Let's sing a song to help us remember how God kept his promise to give Abraham and Sarah a baby.** Teach preschoolers the following words to the tune of "Twinkle, Twinkle, Little Star."

Sing:

**Ha ha, hee hee,** *(hold tummy and pretend to laugh)*

**Let's all laugh.**

**God sent a baby**

**In the past.**

**Abe and Sarah**

**Felt too old**

**To have a baby**

**They could hold.**

**Ha ha, hee hee,** *(hold tummy and pretend to laugh)*

**Let's all laugh.**

**God sent a baby**

**In the past.**

# God's Promise

## Action Play

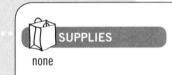

**SUPPLIES**

**R**ead your preschoolers the following rhyme about Abraham and Sarah, having them follow along as you do the actions in parentheses while you read each line.

Rhyme:

**One day three visitors came by.** *(hold up three fingers)*

**Abraham and Sarah smiled and said "Hi!"** *(wave hello)*

**Sarah hurried to make some food.** *(pretend to stir a pot)*

**She cooked it over a fire of wood.** *(pretend to gather wood)*

**The visitors had something big to say.** *(cup your hands around your mouth)*

**They couldn't wait another day.** *(shake your index finger back and forth)*

**In one more year, you'll have a son.** *(hold up one finger)*

**Sarah laughed; she thought it was fun.** *(pretend to laugh)*

**But she had a baby—a boy—it's true!** *(pretend to rock a baby in your arms)*

**God promised a baby, and the promise came true.** *(stretch your arms up high, praising God)*

**SUPPLIES**

## Prayer

**H**ave kids sit in a circle on the floor with you. Start the prayer time by thanking God for Isaac and the happiness he brought to Abraham and Sarah. Then go around the circle and have kids each say the name of someone they're thankful for—someone who makes them happy. Close the prayer by thanking God for each child in your group and the happiness they all bring to you.

# Baby Isaac

**GOD PROMISES ABRAHAM AND SARAH A BABY**   GENESIS 18:1-16; 21:1-7

# God Protects Baby Moses

## Exodus 2

## A Baby by the River

### Bible Experience

**SUPPLIES**

Bible, bedsheet (any size)

**G**ather children in a circle and have them sit down. Turn in your Bible to Exodus 2. Show children the words, and tell them the Bible is God's special book.

Say: **The Bible says a long time ago there was a king who did not love or follow God. He made God's people his servants. They had to work hard for him.**

**The king was worried about God's people becoming stronger than him. So he wanted to get rid of all the baby boys born to God's people.**

**One woman had a baby boy named Moses. She loved him very much.** Bundle the sheet into a "baby" and rock it. Pass the bundle around the circle and let each child hold the "baby." When the bundle comes back to you, hold it.

Ask:

- *What are some ways our parents show they love us?*

Say: **Moses' mother didn't want the king's soldiers to find Moses, so she hid him.** Have children close their eyes while you hide the bundle. See if any children can guess where you've hidden it. Then let the child who found the "baby" hide it. Play a few times; then hold the bundle again.

**As baby Moses grew, he got too big and noisy to hide. So his mother made a special boat out of a basket for him. She put Moses in the basket, and then she put the basket in the water along the edge of the river.** Lay the sheet in the middle of the circle and explain to preschoolers that this is the "river." Let children grab the edges of the sheet and wiggle it to make gentle waves in the river. Then lay the sheet flat.

**Baby Moses had an older sister named Miriam. Miriam hid behind some of the tall grass near the water and watched to see what would happen.** Have children hold their hands in front of their faces, fingers spread as if they're peeking through grass.

**While Miriam was watching Moses, the king's daughter—a princess—went to take a bath in the river.** Let preschoolers sit on the sheet and pretend to take a bath, scrubbing and washing their arms, legs, and hair. **Suddenly the princess saw the floating basket. When she opened it, she saw baby Moses inside. The princess picked Moses up and held him gently.** Have children step off the sheet and sit down around it. Gather the sheet into a bundle again and hold it like a baby.

**The princess wanted to take care of baby Moses, but she wasn't sure how to do that. So Miriam ran to get her mother, who was also baby Moses' mother. And the princess paid baby Moses' mother to take care of him until he was old enough to come live in the palace.**

Have preschoolers jump up and down to cheer for the way God protected baby Moses.

# Basket Boats

## Craft

**SUPPLIES**

foam or paper cups, wax-based modeling clay, cotton balls, smiley-face stickers, bins of water or a water table (optional)

**S**ay: **Moses' mother took care of Moses by making a basket that could float. God watched over baby Moses too by leading the princess to find the basket. Let's make our own basket boats to remember that God watches over us, too.**

Give each child a foam or paper cup. Help preschoolers tear small pieces off the rim of their cups, leaving the cups only about 2 inches tall. These will be their baskets. As preschoolers work, talk about how Moses' mother worked to make a special basket for baby Moses.

Help preschoolers press a small amount of modeling clay into the bottom of the basket. (This adds ballast, keeping the basket from tipping over.) Give each child a cotton ball and talk about how soft a baby's skin is. Then give each child a smiley-face sticker to put on top of the cotton ball for the baby's face.

Let preschoolers put their babies in their baskets. You may want to provide a water table or bins of water so preschoolers can gently float the baskets in the water.

As kids work, discuss the following questions.

Ask:

- *What are ways God keeps us safe?*
- *Who keeps you safe and watches over you today?*

# River Runners

# Game

**SUPPLIES**

plastic spoons, cotton balls, spray bottle filled with water, supplies to make an obstacle course such as chairs, tables, books, and other objects from around the room

**B**efore children arrive, set up a simple "river" obstacle course for children to maneuver through.

Have children form a line at the beginning of the course.

Say: **Let's play a game to remember how Moses' mother loved him and did all she could to keep him safe.**

Provide the first child in line with a cotton ball and a spoon. Tell the group the cotton ball is a little baby and the spoon is a basket. Have children take turns using the "basket" to safely carry the "baby" down the "river." (Show children the obstacles they need to go over, under, or around.) If kids drop the cotton ball, they can pick it up, place it back in the spoon, and keep going. Since they're carrying the baby down a river, let kids know you'll spray them with a water bottle while they race. After everyone has had a turn, lead children in thanking God for those who love us and keep us safe.

# Basket Bites

## Snack

**H**ave children clean their hands, and give each child a plate with a cracker on it. Have children look at the cracker. Point out how the cracker looks like it's woven together like the basket Moses' mother wove to hold Moses while he was in the river.

Then give each child a square of cheese to put on the cracker. Let preschoolers touch the cheese and describe how it feels.

Say: **A baby's skin is soft and smooth—like this cheese. Imagine that baby Moses had cheeks and fingers that might have felt like this.**

Then give each child a few pieces of cucumber-strip grass to place on top of the cheese and cracker. Talk about how Moses' mother put Moses in the tall grass along the edge of the river. And remind children how Miriam—Moses' sister—hid in the grass to see what would happen to Moses.

**God watched over baby Moses. He sent a princess who had a gentle heart and wanted to see the baby grow up to be big and strong.**

Pray and thank God for your snack and for watching over us. Let kids eat and enjoy.

# God Is Watching

## Song

**S**ay: **Let's sing a song to help us remember how God took care of baby Moses.** Teach preschoolers the following words and motions to the tune of "Alouette."

Sing:

**Baby Moses,** *(pretend to rock a baby)*

**Little baby Moses,** *(continue rocking)*

**Baby Moses,** *(continue rocking)*

**Floating in the Nile.** *(use arms to make waves)*

**God is watching,** *(shade eyes with hands and look around)*

**Always, always watching.** *(shade eyes with hands and look around)*

**God is watching,** *(shade eyes with hands and look around)*

**Loving and true!** *(hug self)*

# As You Grow

## Action Play

**SUPPLIES**

**L**ead children in this rhyme about baby Moses in the river, having them follow along as you do the actions in parentheses while you read each line.

Rhyme:

**Tall, tall grass grows** *(crouch down; then "grow" like the tall grass)*

**By the river Nile.** *(make waves with arms)*

**Who do you see hiding there?** *(cover eyes; then uncover them)*

**A fish or crocodile?** *(put hands together to make a swimming fish; then open arms wide and clap them together like a crocodile's jaws)*

**No, it's a sleepy baby** *(rock a baby)*

**In a basket, safe and dry.** *(keep rocking baby)*

**His sister watches from afar,** *(shade eyes with hands)*

**Hoping he won't cry!** *(rub eyes as if crying)*

**Suddenly a splish and splash!** *(fling fingers wide twice)*

**The princess comes to take a bath!** *(rub arms and legs as if bathing)*

**In the tall, tall grass she sees** *(crouch down; then "grow" like the tall grass)*

**The baby sleeping happily.** *(put head on hands as if sleeping)*

**God watched over that baby boy** *(point up)*

**As he grew and grew.** *(crouch down; then "grow" up)*

**God watches over me** *(point to self)*

**And God watches over you!** *(point to a friend)*

# People Prayer

## Prayer

**H**ave preschoolers sit in a circle with you.

Say: **Moses had a mother who loved him and fed him and rocked him to sleep at night.** Have preschoolers put their heads on their hands, as if asleep. **Let's thank God for people who love us.** Go around the circle inviting willing children to take turns saying, "God, thank you for [name], who loves me."

**God gave Moses a sister who watched him while he was in the river.** Have children put their hands above their eyes, as if watching something. **Let's thank God for people who watch over us. Think of a different person than you thought of before.** Go around the circle again, inviting willing children to take turns saying, "God, thank you for [name], who watches over me."

**God sent a princess who was kind to Moses. She took him from the water and gave him a good place to live.** Have kids hug themselves. **Now let's thank God for people who are kind to us. Try to think of someone you haven't thanked God for yet.** Go around the circle one more time, inviting willing children to take turns saying, "God, thank you for [name], who is kind to me."

When kids are done sharing, close the prayer time by having everyone say together, "In Jesus' name, amen."

# God Gives Moses the Ten Commandments

## Exodus 19:3–20:17

## Block Talk

### Bible Experience

**SUPPLIES**

Bible, enough wooden blocks for each child to have at least 2 and enough to make a pile

**G**ather children in a circle and have them sit down. Set aside two blocks per child, and then set a pile of blocks in the middle of the circle. Turn in your Bible to Exodus 19. Show children the words, and tell them the Bible is God's special book.

Say: **In the Bible, God's people were the Israelites. They loved God, but sometimes did things that God didn't want them to do. So God gave them a leader named Moses. God told Moses to meet him up on a mountain. Let's use these blocks to make that mountain.** Let preschoolers stack the blocks into a mountain shape, and then gather everyone around the mountain.

**When God came to the mountain, there were clouds, thunder, and lightning. Let's use our blocks to make thunder.** Give preschoolers each two blocks and have them clap the blocks together.

**Moses climbed the mountain and God talked to him. God gave Moses 10 rules for people to follow. God wrote the rules on stone, and God's rules told people how to live. The first and most important rule was to *only* worship God—he's number one!** Have preschoolers each hold up one block.

**And because they only worshipped God, he told people to never worship other things.** Lead preschoolers in making a tower of blocks and then knocking it down.

**Another rule God gave was to have one special day of rest and worship.** Have kids each take a block to make a pretend pillow for their heads. Have them rest their heads on their pillows to remember God's rule to have one day of rest. Have children "rest" while you continue.

**God wanted his people not to steal or tell lies. God told them to obey their parents and to be happy with what they had.**

Ask:

- *Who makes the rules you follow?*
- *How do rules help us?*
- *What's good about following the rules?*

Say: **God loved his people and wanted them to be safe. His rules helped them. God loves us and wants us to follow his rules, too. His special rules still keep us safe today!**

# Clouds and Mountains

## Craft

**SUPPLIES**

shaving cream, paper towels, wet wipes, smocks (optional)

**G**ather children around a table. (You may want to put a smock on each child, although shaving cream won't harm their clothing.)

Say: **Moses went up a big mountain to hear God give his special rules. When God came near the mountain, there were thick clouds. Today you'll get to play in something that can be like a mountain *or* a cloud!**

Squirt a generous dollop of shaving cream on the table in front of each child. Let children know not to put it in their mouths, and have them scoop it into a mountain shape, making it as tall as possible. Then let preschoolers swirl the shaving cream with their fingers to make fluffy clouds.

**God used his hand to write his rules in stone. You can pretend you're writing God's rules, too.** Help preschoolers smooth the shaving cream in front of them, and then have them each use their finger to "write" or draw God's rules.

Ask:

- *Why is it sometimes hard to follow rules?*

Say: **God's good rules keep us safe. But even when we don't follow them, God still loves us and forgives us.**

Let preschoolers clean the shaving cream from the table and from their hands. Compare cleaning the shaving cream with the way God forgives and cleans our hearts.

# Hop to It
## Game

 **SUPPLIES**

masking tape, music player and upbeat preschool-friendly praise music

**B**efore children arrive, tape several Xs on the floor in a circle about 2 feet apart (you'll need at least one X per child).

Say: **God's rules were so important that he wanted the people to stop what they were doing and listen carefully. Let's play a game to see what that's like.** Have preschoolers each move to an X and stand on it. Play music and have children hop from X to X. When you stop the music, have children stop hopping and listen to your instructions. Give instructions such as:

- hug a friend
- hop to someone wearing blue and say, "You're a good friend."
- clap two times
- give someone a high five
- jump up and down two times
- cheer "God loves us!"

Then repeat the process. After playing several rounds, gather children on the floor.

Ask:

- *When do you have to listen to instructions?*
- *When can it be hard to stop and listen?*

Say: **It's important to listen carefully to God. He loves us and wants what's best for us.**

# Get the Wiggles Out!

## Snack

 **SUPPLIES**

gelatin cups, bear-shaped graham crackers, plastic spoons, non-dairy whipped topping (optional), antibacterial gel (optional)

*ALLERGY ALERT!*
See page 5

**H**ave children clean their hands, and give each child a gelatin cup and a bear-shaped graham cracker to represent Moses. Have children put "Moses" on the gelatin "mountain." Let preschoolers gently shake the cups and watch the gelatin wiggle. Point out that the mountain shook with God's power when he met there with Moses. (You may want to give each child a squirt of whipped topping as a reminder of the clouds that surrounded the mountain.)

Ask:

- *What's it like when you hear thunder or see lightning?*
- *How does it help you to know that God loves you?*

Say: **Even though God has the power to make mountains shake, he loves each one of us in a unique way.**

# Moses Went up the Mountain

## Song

 **SUPPLIES**

**S**ay: **Let's sing a song to help us remember how God gave Moses the Ten Commandments.** Teach preschoolers the following words and motions to the tune of "The Bear Went Over the Mountain."

Sing:

**Moses went up the mountain** (*pretend to climb with arms and legs*)

**Moses went up the mountain** (*pretend to climb with arms and legs*)

**Moses went up the mountain** (*pretend to climb with arms and legs*)

**To hear what God would say.** (*cup hand around one ear*)

**He heard what God did say.** (*cup hand around one ear*)

**He heard what God did say.** (*cup hand around one ear*)

**God had special rules for his people** (*cross hands on chest*)

**Special rules for his people** (*cross hands on chest*)

**Special rules for his people** (*cross hands on chest*)

**To help them do what's right.** (*put thumbs up and nod*)

# God's Rules

## Action Play

SUPPLIES

**L**ead preschoolers in the following rhyme about the Ten Commandments, having them follow along as you do the actions in parentheses while you read each line.

Rhyme:

**Step, step, step go Moses' feet.** *(walk in place)*

**Rumble, rumble; thunder beat.** *(stomp feet to make thunder)*

**Flash of lightning—clouds roll in.** *(fling fingers wide; then move arms in circles)*

**Mountain shakes and God begins.** *(shake hands side to side)*

**"Keep me first, I'm number one.** *(hold up index finger)*

**Idols? Statues? You'll have none.** *(cross arms across chest)*

**The day of rest is made for me.** *(point up)*

**Obey your parents cheerfully."** *(fold hands and smile)*

**"Be happy with the things you have.** *(trace a smile on your face)*

**Lying? Stealing? That's all bad.** *(put thumbs down)*

**Obey my rules—they'll keep you safe.** *(hug yourself and turn shoulders back and forth)*

**And guide you each and every day."** *(walk in place)*

## Prayer

**S**ay: **God's special rules help us follow him, know him, and do things his way. God's first rule was to pray only to him and worship only him. Let's use our feet as we talk to God, just as Moses did.**

Have children take one giant step forward. Then have them each thank God for something that's important to them by saying, "Thank you, God, for…" and naming something, such as their families, their health, food, a pet, or the home they live in. If you have a larger group, children can pray silently.

Next, direct children to take a tiny step forward. Invite them each to pray for something that's hard or that they're afraid to do by saying, "Help me, God, to…" and naming something, such as being kind to brothers and sisters, telling the truth, or sharing with others. Allow time for children to pray.

Finally, lead preschoolers in hopping forward three times. Give each child the chance to complete the sentence "God you are…" with something that's wonderful about God.

When kids are done sharing, close by having everyone say together, "In Jesus' name, amen."

# God Hears Hannah's Prayer

## 1 Samuel 1:1–2:2

## What Do You Hear?

### Bible Experience

**SUPPLIES**

Bible

**G**ather children together and have them sit in a circle with you. Open your Bible to 1 Samuel, and show children the words. Tell them the Bible is God's special book.

Say: **The Bible tells about a woman named Hannah who didn't have any children. Hannah was married, and her husband loved her very much. But because she wanted a child and didn't have one, she was very sad.**

Ask:

- *Tell about a time you were sad because you wanted something but couldn't have it.*

Say: **Every year Hannah and her husband traveled to a city called Shiloh to worship God.** Have children walk in place while you continue to talk. **One year while they were in Shiloh, Hannah went away to pray by herself.** Have children get on their knees as if they're praying while you continue to talk. **Hannah was so sad about not having a child that she cried as she prayed.**

Ask:

- *Tell about a time you wanted something so badly that you cried when you asked for it.*

Say: **Hannah also made a promise to God that if he gave her a son, she'd make sure her son served God his whole life.**

Ask:

- *Tell about a time you made a promise to do something if you got what you wanted.*

Say: **When Hannah prayed, she moved her lips but she didn't make any sounds. She was praying in her heart.** Have kids try saying, "My name is [child's name]" with their lips without making any sounds.

Ask:

- *How easy was it to understand others when they just moved their lips but didn't make any sounds?*

Say: **There was a man named Eli—a priest—who saw Hannah praying. And he thought something was wrong because he saw her lips moving but didn't hear anything.**

Ask:

- *Tell about a time you couldn't tell what someone was saying.*

Say: **When Eli realized Hannah was praying in her heart and found out what she was praying for, he comforted Hannah and also prayed that God would give her a baby. And Hannah was no longer sad after that because she believed God heard her prayer.**

**And God *did* hear her prayer. A short time later, Hannah had a son named Samuel. And Hannah praised God for the way he had answered her prayer.** Have kids jump and cheer for God. **And just as Hannah promised, she made sure Samuel served God his whole life.**

# Prayerful Hands

## Craft

**SUPPLIES**

construction paper, pen or pencil, scissors, crayons, stickers (optional)

**Teacher TIP**

If you have a large group, you may want to ask another adult for help tracing and cutting in this activity.

**T**race each child's hands—palms down with thumbs touching—on a sheet of construction paper. Cut around the outside edges of the hands, leaving the thumbs connected. Then fold the hands together, forming a crease where the thumbs meet.

Allow children to color or place stickers on the outside of the hands. On the inside of the hands, have children draw pictures of things to pray to God about.

Let children take their prayerful hands home as a reminder that God always listens to their prayers.

# Listen Before You Step!

## Game

**SUPPLIES**

paper, blindfolds

**S**catter crumpled pieces of paper around an area of the floor. Have children form a line off to one side of the paper. Tell kids they have to walk through the papers—blindfolded—without stepping on any of them. Explain that they can ask you where to go, and you'll always answer when they ask. Have kids go one or two at a time so you're able to give them instructions when they ask. Give kids only one or two instructions at a time, and wait until they ask for more.

When the game is over, talk about how important it was for them to ask you for help so they wouldn't step on the papers. Point out that it's also important for us to ask God when we need his help.

Ask:

- *What are some things you can ask God to help you with?*
- *What did you like about the way I responded when you asked for help?*
- *How do you know God always hears you when you ask for his help?*

Say: **God wants to help us, so don't be afraid to talk to him the next time you need help.**

# Prayer Snack Mix

## Snack

**SUPPLIES**

pretzel twists, an assortment of dried fruit, Hershey's Kisses, resealable plastic bags, napkins, antibacterial gel (optional)

*ALLERGY ALERT!*
See page 5

**H**ave children clean their hands, and provide each child with a small quantity of each ingredient on a napkin, one item at a time. As you hand out the pretzel twists, point out that they look like arms folded in prayer and remind us to pray. Have kids each hold a pretzel while a few willing kids pray. Distribute the dried fruit, and tell kids it can remind us of all God has provided for us. Ask kids to name some things God has provided. Finally, distribute the Hershey's Kisses and tell kids the candies remind us of God's love. Ask kids to share ways they know God loves them.

Have children each put their ingredients in a resealable plastic bag. Help kids seal their bags and mix up the ingredients, and then let kids eat and enjoy.

# God Hears My Prayers

## Song

**SUPPLIES**

**S**ay: **Let's sing a song about how God hears and answers our prayers just like he did for Hannah.** Teach preschoolers the following words and motions to the tune of "Give Me Oil in My Lamp."

Sing:

**God hears my prayers 'cause he loves me.** *(cup a hand around your ear)*

**God hears my prayers 'cause he cares.** *(give yourself a hug)*

**God hears my prayers 'cause he loves me, loves me, loves me,** *(cup a hand around your ear)*

**And he knows just what it is I need.** *(point index finger to forehead, and then point to yourself)*

**God answers prayers 'cause he's listening.** *(cup a hand around your ear.)*

**God answers prayers 'cause he cares.** *(give yourself a hug)*

**God answers prayers 'cause he's listening, listening, listening,** *(cup a hand around your ear)*

**And he knows just what it is I need.** *(point index finger to forehead, and then point to yourself)*

# Hannah's Prayer

## Action Play

**SUPPLIES**

Lead preschoolers in the following rhyme about Hannah's prayer, having them follow along as you do the actions in parentheses while you read each line.

Rhyme:

**Hannah prayed to God,** *(touch palms together)*

**"Please give me a son.** *(rock a baby back and forth)*

**And if you do,** *(point index finger up)*

**I will give him back to you."** *(hold hands out in front, palms up)*

**Hannah prayed to God,** *(touch palms together)*

**"Please give me a son.** *(rock a baby back and forth)*

**I will not cut his hair.** *(make scissors with fingers and pretend to cut)*

**Wouldn't that be fair?"** *(hold hands out to side, palms up)*

**Hannah had a son.** *(rock a baby back and forth)*

**She named him Samuel.** *(continue rocking)*

**She gave him to the Lord,** *(hold hands out in front, palms up)*

**Praising God for her reward.** *(put arms in the air and wiggle hands)*

**God heard Hannah's prayer.** *(cup hand to ear)*

**I can pray to God, too.** *(point to self)*

**God hears what I say,** *(cup hand to ear)*

**He'll hear what you say, too.** *(point to another person)*

# Heart Prayers

## Prayer

**H**ave children sit in a circle. Sing the following prayer to the tune of "Mary Had a Little Lamb."

Sing:

**God listens to all our prayers, all our prayers, all our prayers;**

**God listens to all our prayers.**

**Let's bow our heads and pray.**

Remind children that Hannah's prayer was silent because she was praying in her heart. Allow time for children to quietly pray in their hearts just as Hannah did.

After kids have had time to pray in their hearts, close the time with the following prayer:

Pray:

**Thank you, God, for listening to the prayer in Hannah's heart and for listening to the prayers in our hearts, too. In Jesus' name, amen.**

# God Chooses David

## 1 Samuel 16:1-13

## Who Will Be King?

### Bible Experience

**SUPPLIES**

Bible, bottle of oil (any kind of non-toxic oil is fine), random objects from around the room

**H**ave children sit in a circle with you. Open your Bible to 1 Samuel 16, and show children the words. Tell them the Bible is God's special book.

Say: **The Bible tells how David was chosen to be king of Israel. King Saul wasn't a good king. He didn't follow God. So God decided to make someone else king in Saul's place.**

**God knew who he wanted to be king, and God sent Samuel to find that person. God told Samuel it would be one of Jesse's sons, who lived near Bethlehem. God told Samuel to find Jesse. God would show Samuel which son would be the new king.**

Play a quick game of I Spy with your group. Identify something small in the room you want children to find. Say: **I spy something** [descriptor of the item, such as color, size, or shape]. Have children guess by going to an item and bringing it to you. After two or three incorrect guesses, give another descriptor of the item. Continue until someone guesses correctly. If time allows, play the game two or three times. When the game is over, have children sit in a circle again.

Ask:

- *How was our game like Samuel looking for God's new king?*

Say: **When Samuel arrived in Bethlehem, Jesse introduced Samuel to his seven sons. When Samuel met the first son, Samuel thought he looked like the type of man who would make a good king.**

Ask:

- *What do you think a king might look like?*

Say: **God told Samuel that Jesse's first son wasn't the king. God doesn't care about what a person looks like on the outside; God cares about what a person is like in his or her heart.**

Ask:

- *What do you think God wants us to be like in our hearts?*

Say: **Samuel went on to meet another of Jesse's sons. He wasn't the one God had chosen, either. In fact, God didn't choose any of the seven brothers.**

**Since Samuel hadn't found the new king, he asked Jesse if these were all his children. Jesse said there was still one more son—the youngest, David—who was taking care of the sheep.** Have children make sheep sounds. **Samuel had Jesse get David. When Samuel met David, God told Samuel that David was his choice to be the new king. David had the kinds of things in his heart God was looking for. So Samuel put oil on David's head in front of David's whole family to show that God had chosen David.** Show kids the bottle of oil. **From that day on, God's Spirit was with David in a special way.**

Ask:

- *Tell about a time someone chose you to do something special.*
- *What was it like for you to be chosen?*

Say: **God has special plans for you, too. We just need to listen and obey him to find out what those plans are.**

# What's on the Inside

## Craft

**SUPPLIES**

enough craft foam to make a crown for each child, washable markers, heart stickers, yarn, scissors, hole punch

**B**efore children arrive, cut craft foam to resemble a crown and punch a hole at each end. You'll need to make one crown for each child. Say: **What was inside David's heart was more important to God than what David looked like on the outside. Let's make something to remind us that God cares about our hearts, too.**

Give each child a craft-foam crown. Set out markers, and let kids decorate the outside of their crowns in any way they choose. Then give kids each a heart sticker to put on the inside of their crowns. Help children each tie a piece of yarn through the holes at each end of their crown so the crowns fit on their heads. As children work, ask the following questions.

Ask:

- *What ways can we have a heart that makes God happy?*
- *Why do you think God cares more about who we are in our hearts than what we look like on the outside?*

Say: **When you wear your crown, remember that even though it looks great on the outside, the most important thing about it is the heart on the inside.**

# What's Inside?

## Game

Place one object in each bag and close the bag so children can't see inside. Let children take turns reaching inside each bag and guessing what the objects are by feeling them but not looking at them. When kids are done guessing, show them the object in each bag.

Say: **God told Samuel we see people based on how they look on the outside, but God knows what people are like in their hearts.**

Ask:

- *What was it like feeling inside the bags?*
- *Explain whether the artwork on the outside of each bag helped you know what was inside the bag.*

Say: **The objects in the bags each felt different when you touched them. What our hearts are like is often different from what we look like on the outside.**

# What Goes Inside
# Makes a Difference

## Snack

**B**efore children arrive, set out two mixing bowls. Next to one bowl set the butter, sugar, vanilla, flour, and chocolate chips. Next to the other bowl set the dirt, grass, rocks, dead leaves, and sticks.

Say: **God knew David had a good heart and that David loved God. Having a good heart means we love God and make good choices. Let's make a snack that reminds us of this.**

Have kids clean their hands and then gather around the mixing bowls and ingredients. Ask children for examples of good choices and bad choices. If children are too young, give examples of good and bad choices (lying, praying, stealing, being kind, and so on). For every good choice mentioned, put a good ingredient (butter, sugar, vanilla, flour, chocolate chips—in that order) into the "good" mixing bowl. For every bad choice mentioned, put a bad ingredient (dirt, grass, rocks, dead leaves, sticks) into the "bad" mixing bowl. Use a different hand for adding each batch of ingredients, stirring as you go. Once all the ingredients are added and mixed, let children see the difference in the contents of each bowl.

Give each child a portion of cookie dough on a paper plate. (If you have a large group, increase the recipe accordingly.) Let kids eat and enjoy. As kids are eating, ask the following questions.

Ask:

- *How are the good things we put in the mixing bowl like the goodness in our hearts?*
- *What do you think would happen to the cookie dough if you put just one of the bad ingredients into it?*

Say: **Even when bad things get into our hearts, God still loves us. He can clean the bad things out. Let's make good choices so we can have good hearts just like David.**

# He's Deep Down in My Heart
## Song

SUPPLIES
none

**S**ay: **Let's sing a song to help us remember how God chose David.** Teach preschoolers the following words to the tune of "He's Got the Whole World in His Hands."

Sing:

**God knows how much I love him, in my heart.**

**Yes, he knows how much I love him, in my heart.**

**God knows how much I love him, in my heart.**

**I love him deep down in my heart.**

**I'll never be lonely 'cause he's in my heart.**

**No, I'll never be lonely 'cause he's in my heart.**

**I'll never be lonely 'cause he's in my heart.**

**God is deep down in my heart.**

# Samuel Went to Bethlehem
## Action Play

SUPPLIES
none

**R**ead your preschoolers the following rhyme about God choosing David to be king, having them follow along as you do the actions in parentheses while you read each line.

Rhyme:

**Old Samuel went to Bethlehem** *(walk in place)*

**To find himself a king.** *(cup hands around top of head as if putting on a crown)*

**"Don't worry how he looks outside,"** *(circle face with open hands, palms forward)*

**God said, "His heart's the thing."** *(place hands on heart)*

**Seven brothers Samuel met.** *(hold up seven fingers)*

**But God said, "You're not done."** *(shake head no)*

**When David came in from the fields,** *(wave)*

**God told him, "He's the one!"** *(thrust pointer finger forward)*

# David's Prayer

## Prayer

**S**ay: **In the Bible, David wrote a prayer asking God to look at his heart. That's one way David made sure he had the good heart God wanted.** Paraphrase Psalm 139:23-24 for kids, having them follow along as you do the motions in parentheses as you read each line.

Read:

**"Search me, O God, and know my heart;** *(place hands on heart)*

**Test me and know my worried thoughts.** *(touch index fingers to temples)*

**Point out anything in me that upsets you,** *(point to self; then point up)*

**and lead me along the path of life forever with you."** *(walk in place)*

After reading and acting out this verse, read through it again as a way for kids to pray. This time, allow time after reading it for kids to pray quietly. Kids can ask God to help them make good choices and remind them that he cares about their hearts, not what's on the outside.

Close the time by praying aloud, asking God to show everyone how to have a good heart in God's sight.

# God Helps David Defeat Goliath

## 1 Samuel 17:12-51

## David's Bravery

### Bible Experience

**SUPPLIES**

Bible, blocks, tape measure, a bulky or heavy item such as a full backpack that is too heavy for preschoolers to lift but not too heavy for you, 2 adult-sized button-up shirts, 2 pairs of adult shoes

**H**ave children sit in a circle with you. Open your Bible to 1 Samuel 17, and show children the words. Tell them the Bible is God's special book.

Say: **The Bible tells about a fight between a shepherd boy and a giant. Their names were David and Goliath. David's people—the Israelites—were at war with Goliath's people—the Philistines. Goliath was the champion of the Philistines. He was 9 feet tall!** Have a willing child lie on the floor. Place a block by the child's feet and one by the child's head to mark his or her height. Do the same thing with yourself or another adult. Then stretch the tape measure to 9 feet and place it next to the blocks to show how tall Goliath was. Have kids take turns lying down in each measurement so they can see how they measure up.

**Every morning and every evening Goliath would challenge the Israelites to send one soldier to fight against him. But the men of Israel were too scared to go.**

Ask:

- *Tell about a time you were scared to do something.*

Say: **One day David came to the Israelite camp to bring some food to his brothers. While he was there, he heard the challenge Goliath made to the Israelites. David knew that Goliath wasn't just challenging the army of Israel, he was challenging God, too. And that upset David. So David decided he would take Goliath's challenge to fight.**

**Everyone else thought David was too young to fight Goliath.**

Ask:

- *What are some things people might think you're too young to do?*

Say: **David had already fought against bears and lions when he was watching his father's sheep, so he wasn't afraid. But more importantly, he knew God was on his side. Let's see why that's important.** Have kids take turns trying to pick up the heavy object. After each child has tried to lift the object, offer to help him or her lift the item off the ground. Point out that when God is on our side, we can do things we can't do all on our own. And David knew God would help him.

**King Saul agreed to let David fight Goliath. But the king wanted David to wear his suit of armor and use his sword.** Have kids form two lines, and have the first child in each line put on an adult-sized shirt and shoes. Then have the two kids try to cross the room and come back, where they'll give the shirt and shoes to the next person in line. Play until all kids have had a turn shuffling across the room.

**King Saul's armor and sword were too big for David. So instead David used the things he was used to—his stick, his sling, and five smooth stones.** Have kids form two lines again and this time race back and forth across the room without the burden of the too-large shirts and shoes.

Ask:

- *When was it easier to cross the room—wearing grown-up clothes or wearing your own clothes? Why?*

Say: **When Goliath saw David coming to fight him, he laughed. He thought it was silly to think that a young boy could beat a giant soldier. He said a lot of mean things to David just because David was small. He wanted to scare David. But David didn't give up. David told Goliath he wasn't afraid of Goliath's huge sword and spear because David came in the name of the Lord God. And he knew God was more powerful than any giant.**

**Goliath started to walk toward David, so David ran toward Goliath.** Have kids run in place. **David took a stone out of his bag, put it into his sling, and spun his sling around.** Have kids pretend to take a stone out of a bag, put it in a sling, and spin the sling around. **And when the stone came out, it hit Goliath right on the head and knocked him down.** Have kids pretend to throw a stone from a sling and then fall to the ground. **David won! He was brave because he knew God was with him. And because of his bravery, the army of Israel was saved.** Have kids jump and cheer.

THE **GIANT** BOOK OF PRESCHOOL IDEAS FOR CHILDREN'S MINISTRY

# Pompom Launchers

## Craft

**S**ay: **David used his sling to help protect his family's sheep, so he was good at using it. Let's make something to remember that when David fought Goliath, he used something that was familiar to him—a sling and five smooth stones.**

Give each child a rubber band and five pompoms to represent David and his five stones.

Show children how to hold a rubber band between thumb and forefinger and then put a pompom in the rubber band "sling." Help children pull and release the rubber band to launch the pompoms at a bucket or bowl. Show kids how to hold their launchers and continue trying to hit a target with a pompom.

Ask:

- *Explain whether you think this was easy or difficult to do.*
- *What are some things you're good at?*
- *God used David's skill with a sling to help free his people. How could God use something you're good at to do something for him?*

# Sticky Goliath

## Game

**S**ay: **David used a sling and five smooth stones to fight Goliath. I bet he had to practice a lot to have such good aim. Let's practice and see if we can make our stones stick to a target.**

Hang the fleece or felt pieces on a wall about 3 feet off the floor. Have children form two lines about 5 feet away from the wall. Give the first child in each line a bowl with five Velcro balls in it. These balls are their stones. Have children take turns throwing the five stones to stick to the target.

# Five Little Stones

## Snack

**S**ay: King Saul wanted David to wear heavy armor to fight Goliath. Instead David chose five stones and a sling. He was very brave because he trusted God. Let's make doughnut holes look like David's stones to remind *us* to always trust God, too.

Have children clean their hands. Give each child two doughnut holes on a paper plate along with a plastic knife and a dollop of chocolate frosting. Help children spread chocolate frosting on their doughnut holes. Set out several plates with chocolate sprinkles, and have kids roll their doughnut holes in the sprinkles. As kids eat, have them talk about why they trust God.

# I May Be Little, but I'm Brave With God

## Song

**S**ay: David was brave when he fought Goliath because he trusted God. Let's sing a song about how trusting God can make us brave, too. Teach kids the following words and motions to the tune of "She'll be Coming 'Round the Mountain."

Sing:

**Even though I'm young and small, I'm brave with God.** *(point to self; then flex arms)*

**Even though I'm young and small, I'm brave with God.** *(point to self; then flex arms)*

**Even when I'm scared and lonely, God will be there for me only.** *(wrap arms around body; then point up)*

**And I know that God will always make me brave.** *(point up; then point to self and flex arms)*

# David and the Giant

## Action Play

**R**ead preschoolers the following rhyme about David and Goliath, having them follow along as you do the actions in parentheses while you read each line.

Rhyme:

**God chose David** *(point finger up)*

**Even though he was small.** *(put hands close to the ground, palms down)*

**Goliath was a giant** *(reach hands above head)*

**Who was nine feet tall.** *(stand on tiptoes)*

**"Fight this giant man," God said,** *(hold fists in front and move arms back and forth)*

**"And trust me in the fight."** *(point up)*

**David tried on armor,** *(pretend to put pants on)*

**But it wasn't very light.** *(sag shoulders)*

**David took the armor off** *(pretend to take pants off)*

**And headed to a brook.** *(walk in place)*

**Five smooth stones went in his sack,** *(hold up five fingers)*

**And his knees, they never shook.** *(shake knees)*

**David threw with all his might.** *(move arm in a throwing motion)*

**Goliath fell right down.** *(fall to the floor; then stand up)*

**God had helped to win the fight.** *(point up with both fingers; then pump arms over head)*

**With a victory, David was crowned.** *(cup both hands on head like a crown)*

**SUPPLIES**

## Prayer

**R**emind children that although David was small, with God's help he was brave. Talk about how God has given us friends and family to help us be brave.

Have children sit in a circle with you. Link arms together and say the following prayer, allowing children to repeat the words.

Pray:

**Thank you, God, for making me brave. Thank you for friends and family who encourage me. Thank you for taking care of me. Help me trust in you. In Jesus' name, amen.**

# God Sends Ravens to Bring Food to Elijah

## 1 Kings 17:1-6

## As God Commands

### Bible Experience

**O**pen your Bible to 1 Kings 17, and show children the words. Tell them the Bible is God's special book. Help kids pair up and get ready to act out the events in 1 Kings 17:1-6.

Say: **The Bible tells about a wicked king named Ahab. Because of all the bad things Ahab had done, God sent the prophet Elijah to give King Ahab a message—there'd be no more rain for the next few years.** Have one child in each pair be "Elijah" and the other "King Ahab." Have Elijah tell King Ahab it won't rain for several years. Instruct King Ahab to cross his or her arms and look angry.

**Then God sent Elijah away from King Ahab. God sent him to hide near a stream where he would have water to drink. God also promised to send birds called ravens to bring Elijah food.** The child who was King Ahab before will now play the role of God. Have God tell Elijah to go hide near the stream and wait for birds to bring him food. Instruct Elijah to pretend to sit near an imaginary stream, drink water, and wait for food.

Say: **Just as he promised, God sent ravens to bring Elijah bread and meat**

**each morning and each evening.** The children who played God will now be the ravens. Have the ravens pretend to bring bread and meat for Elijah to eat. Instruct Elijah to accept the food thankfully and pretend to eat.

Ask:

- *How has God provided for you?*

Say: **Elijah obeyed God, and everything happened the way God said it would. God kept the rain from falling. Elijah was safe. And God provided Elijah with food to eat and water to drink.** Have kids jump up and down and shout, "Yay, God!"

# Paper Ravens

## Craft

**SUPPLIES**

6-inch squares of black construction paper, 2-inch squares of orange construction paper, glue sticks, white crayons

**G**ive each child one black and one orange construction-paper square.

Say: **God told the ravens to take food to Elijah. Let's make paper ravens to remember that we obey God.**

Help preschoolers each make a paper bird using the following instructions. Make sure kids have completed each step before moving to the next one.

1. Tear the black paper into a circle.

2. Fold the black circle in half.

3. Tear the orange paper into a triangle.

4. Fold the orange triangle in half.

5. Matching the folds, glue the triangle inside the circle, letting just a little of the triangle stick out at the top to resemble a beak.

6. Use a white crayon to draw eyes and wings on each side of the bird.

As children color their birds, discuss the following questions.

Ask:

- *What are some ways even animals need to obey?*
- *Why do you think it's important to do what God tells us to do?*

# God Says

## Game

**SUPPLIES**

**S**ay: **The Bible tells us Elijah obeyed God but Ahab didn't. Ahab's disobedience was why God stopped the rain.**

**Let's play a game to remember how to obey God. I'll tell you something to do. If I say "God says," do what I tell you. If I don't say "God says," stand still and wait for me to say something else.**

Give the following instructions, doing the motions yourself whether you say "God says" or not.

Say:

- **God says "Go talk to King Ahab."** *(walk in place)*
- **Make rain.** *(wiggle fingers, moving them up and down to look like rain)*
- **God says "Hide."** *(duck down and hold your hands over your head)*
- **God says "Drink water from the brook."** *(kneel down and pretend to scoop up water to drink)*
- **Go find your own food.** *(walk in place)*
- **God says "Take food to Elijah."** *(flap arms like wings)*

Ask:

- *How well did you obey in this game?*
- *How well do you obey God?*
- *What can make it hard to obey God?*

# Bread and Meat

## Snack

**SUPPLIES**

Vienna sausages cut into small pieces, crackers, large bowl of water, small paper cups, paper plates, towel, antibacterial gel (optional)

ALLERGY ALERT!
See page 5

**H**ave kids clean their hands.

Say: **When God told Elijah to hide from King Ahab, he told him to stay by a stream. This stream provided water for Elijah to drink. Let's pretend to get water from a stream like Elijah did.** Set the bowl of water on a towel. Give each child a cup, and help kids scoop water from the bowl as if scooping it from a stream.

**God also provided food for Elijah. He sent ravens to bring him bread and meat.** Put a few Vienna sausage pieces and a few crackers on a paper plate for each child. Let children take turns delivering a snack plate to another child in the group as a reminder of how the ravens took food to Elijah. When all the kids have food in front of them, thank God for providing the snack and let kids eat. As kids eat, have them share ways God provides for us.

# God Helped Elijah

## Song

**S**ay: **Let's sing a song about how God took care of Elijah when he hid by the stream.** Teach preschoolers the following words and motions to the tune of "Mary Had a Little Lamb."

Sing:

**When Elijah wasn't safe,** *(move pointer finger back and forth)*

**God helped him** *(point up)*

**Hide away.** *(hold hands over head to hide)*

**When Elijah wasn't safe** *(move pointer finger back and forth)*

**He hid beside a stream.** *(hold hands in front and move them side to side while wiggling fingers)*

**God took care of Elijah.** *(point up)*

**Gave him food** *(bring hand to mouth as if eating)*

**And a drink.** *(bring cupped hands to mouth)*

**God took care of Elijah;** *(point up)*

**Birds brought him food to eat.** *(flap arms like a bird)*

# Kept Safe

## Action Play

SUPPLIES
none

**R**ead your preschoolers the following rhyme about Elijah, having them follow along as you do the actions in parentheses while you read each line.

Rhyme:

**God said, "Go tell King Ahab,** *(cup hands to mouth)*

**There will be no more rain.** *(shake finger back and forth)*

**Now hide by the stream** *(hold hands over head as if hiding)*

**Where I will keep you safe."** *(wrap arms around body and turn shoulders back and forth)*

**"The stream will give you water.** *(bring cupped hands to mouth)*

**Birds will bring you food.** *(bring hand to mouth as if eating)*

**You did what I told you.** *(give two thumbs up)*

**Now I will protect you."** *(hug self)*

# Prayer Circle

## Prayer

SUPPLIES
none

**H**ave kids sit in a circle on the floor. Stand outside the circle.

Say: **God provided food and water for Elijah. He provides good things for us, too. Let's thank him for some of the things he's given us.** Allow time for kids to think of something they're thankful for. Invite willing children to complete the sentence "Thank you, God, for…" by walking around the circle and tapping kids' shoulders in any order you choose. Give each child the opportunity to pray. If a child doesn't want to pray aloud, move on to another child.

Close the time by thanking God for each child in the group.

# Elijah and the Woman of Zarephath

## 1 Kings 17:7-16

## God Promises Enough

### Bible Experience

**SUPPLIES**

Bible, sticks or craft sticks, enough plastic food so each child has a piece

**B**efore children arrive, hide two or three pieces of plastic food somewhere in the room.

Gather children in a circle with you. Open your Bible to 1 Kings 17, and show children the words. Tell them the Bible is God's special book.

Say: **The Bible tells about a time God used a woman who didn't have much food to provide Elijah something to eat.**

**The woman lived in a city called Zarephath. God told Elijah to go there and find this woman.** Have children walk in place.

**When Elijah found the woman, she was picking up sticks to make a fire so she could fix a meal for herself and her son.** Have kids pick up sticks and pretend to build a fire.

**Elijah went to the woman and asked her for some water to drink and some bread to eat. But the woman told Elijah she only had enough food for herself and her son. It hadn't rained for a long time, so she couldn't grow any more food to eat. And after they ate this last meal, their food would be all gone.** Have children search the room to find the plastic food you hid earlier. When kids have found all the pieces, ask them to try to share it so that everyone has a piece of the food. Help kids discover that there's not enough food for everyone to eat, just as Elijah and the woman experienced.

**But God gave Elijah a message for the woman. God promised the woman she'd always have enough oil and flour to make bread until it rained again. Elijah told the woman to bake him some bread first and said she would still have enough oil and flour to make bread for herself and her son as well.** Have kids pretend to make bread.

Ask:

- *How do we know we can trust God?*

Say: **And God did exactly what he promised. The woman gave food to Elijah and still had enough food for herself and her son to eat for many days.** Hand out pieces of plastic food to the rest of the children so that each child has something. Then have children jump up and down and thank God that everyone has food to eat.

# Shaping Bread

## Craft

**SUPPLIES**

flour, salt, water, cooking oil, a measuring cup, measuring spoons, large mixing bowl, wooden spoon, wax paper, resealable plastic bags, antibacterial gel (optional)

ALLERGY ALERT!
See page 5

**S**ay: **God sent Elijah to a woman who baked bread for him to eat. God promised she would always have enough food to eat. The woman used flour and oil to make the bread. Let's mix some play dough and shape it into bread to remember that we can always trust God to provide for us.**

Have kids clean their hands. Let kids take turns measuring out ingredients and adding them to the bowl: 3 cups of flour, 4 tablespoons of salt, 1 cup of cold water, and 2 tablespoons of cooking oil. Mix all the ingredients thoroughly; then give each child a piece of wax paper and a chunk of the dough to knead. Invite kids to shape their dough into bread just as the woman in the Bible did

Store each child's piece of dough in a resealable plastic bag to take home and play with.

# How Much Is Enough?

## Game

**SUPPLIES**

**H**ave kids line up side by side facing you.

Say: **I'm going to name some things that require a certain amount to be enough. When I do, show me how much is enough by bunny hopping toward me that number of times. For example, if I say "shoes," you'll hop two times toward me, because two shoes are enough for your feet.**

Read the following list, letting kids hop after you read the name of each item. (Their responses don't always have to be the same.)

Say:

- **shirts**
- **pillows**
- **socks**
- **pancakes**
- **houses**
- **pets**
- **toothbrushes**
- **green beans**

Say: **The woman knew there wasn't enough to eat, just like you know one sock isn't enough for two feet. But Elijah told her there'd be enough. God made the flour and oil last so Elijah, the woman, and her son could eat. Yay, God!** Have children clap and cheer for God.

# The Hungry Teacher

## Snack

**SUPPLIES**

large box of raisins, 3 raisins per child in resealable plastic bags, antibacterial gel (optional)

ALLERGY ALERT!
See page 5

**G**ather kids. Have kids clean their hands, and give each child a resealable plastic bag with three raisins. Keep the box of raisins hidden out of sight.

Say: **Those raisins are making me hungry. I didn't get any.** [Child's name]**, will you share your raisins with me? I promise there'll be enough for everyone.** Ask two or three children this question until one of them shares with you. Thank any children who share.

After a child shares with you—or if no one shares after you've asked two or three children—assure them there will be enough for everyone.

Say: **I promised there would be enough, and I'm keeping that promise.** Get out the box of raisins, and put a snack portion into each child's plastic bag. Let kids eat and enjoy.

As kids eat, ask them about their favorite foods God provides for them. Point out that the woman Elijah met feared there wouldn't be enough food. God promised there *would* be enough. And God kept his promise. The flour and oil did not run out until it rained and the crops grew again.

# God Will Make It Last

## Song

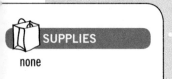

**SUPPLIES**

Say: **Let's sing a song about God providing enough food for Elijah, the woman, and her son.** Teach kids the following words to the tune of "The Farmer in the Dell." If there's roughly an even number of boys and girls in the group, have the boys sing the first verse, the girls sing the second verse, and everyone sing the third verse.

Sing:

**"Bring me a little bread.**

**Bring me a little bread.**

**I need some food to eat.**

**Please bring some water, too."**


**"I don't have any bread.**

**I don't have any bread.**

**I only have some flour and oil,**

**But not enough for you."**


**"Yes, there will be enough.**

**Yes, there will be enough.**

**Our God will make it last,**

**And we will make it through."**

# Making It Last

## Action Play

**SUPPLIES**

**R**ead your preschoolers the following rhyme about Elijah and the woman of Zarephath, having them follow along as you do the actions in parentheses while you read each line.

Rhyme:

**God sent Elijah to Zarephath** *(point finger to something far away)*

**To ask a woman on his path** *(walk in place)*

**For food to eat and water to drink.** *(bring hand to mouth as if eating; then bring cupped hand to mouth)*

**Elijah had some time to think.** *(point to head)*

**He asked the woman for some bread.** *(clasp hands in front)*

**"I have no bread," the woman said.** *(put hands to side, palms up)*

**"My cupboard's bare, I don't have much—** *(shake head side to side)*

**A handful of flour, and oil and such."** *(cup hands in front, palms up)*

**"Don't be concerned," Elijah said.** *(sweep hands away, palms down)*

**"Bake a little loaf of bread.** *(pretend to mix with a spoon)*

**But first, bring some food for me,** *(walk in place)*

**And God's provision you will see."** *(point up)*

**The woman was soon shocked to see** *(raise eyebrows and place hands on cheeks)*

**God's great generosity,** *(put hands to sides, palms up)*

**God supplied her with oil and flour for bread** *(cup hands in front, palms up)*

**Just the way Elijah had said.** *(give two thumbs up)*

# Prayer

**SUPPLIES**

plastic food

**S**ay: **The woman gave Elijah the last of the food she had because she trusted God to provide more for her and her son. Let's give God all that we have, trusting that he'll provide for us, too.**

Have kids sit in a circle. Give each child a piece of plastic food. Invite each child to place his or her plastic food in a pile at the center and pray, "I trust you, God, to provide everything I need."

Close the prayer time by thanking God that we can trust him to provide. Then have the group say together, "In Jesus' name, amen."

# God Uses Elijah to Challenge False Prophets

## 1 Kings 18:1, 17-39

## Fire From God

### Bible Experience

**SUPPLIES**

Bible; building blocks; red, orange, and yellow streamers for each child

**H**ave kids sit in a circle. Open your Bible to 1 Kings 18, and show kids the words. Tell kids the Bible is God's special book.

Say: **The Bible tells about a time Elijah proved to the Israelites that his God was the only true God.**

**King Ahab made Israel worship a false god called Baal. To show that Baal was not real, Elijah had the people build a pile of stones with wood on top, called an altar. Then Elijah built another altar.** Have kids use blocks to build two altars.

**Elijah presented the people with a challenge. They would each pray to their god—the people would pray to Baal and Elijah would pray to the Lord—and whichever god set an altar on fire would be the one true God.** Give children each a red, orange, and yellow streamer to hold. Have children gather around the first altar and hold their streamers behind their backs. Tell them to pretend to be fire waiting to light one of the altars.

Elijah had the people who worshipped Baal pray for Baal to set their altar on fire. These people spent all day asking Baal for fire. They shouted. They danced. They cried. But nothing happened. When they were so tired they couldn't do anything else, Elijah called everyone over to the altar he had built. Invite kids to move to the second altar.

Elijah prayed to the Lord for fire, but he only had to ask one time. He prayed, "O Lord, answer me! Answer me so these people will know that you, O Lord, are God." Right away, fire fell from heaven and burned up the altar. Invite kids to walk around the altar, waving their streamers and pretending to burn up everything near the altar.

Ask:

- *What does this tell us about God's power?*

Say: **When the Lord's people saw the fire, they knew there was only one God. They shouted, "The Lord is God!" Let's shout that, too!** Let kids continue to wave their streamers as they shout, "The Lord is God!"

# Building an Altar

## Craft

**SUPPLIES**

sheets of gray construction paper trimmed round to resemble stones, crayons

**G**ive each child a sheet of gray construction paper. Point out that the paper looks like the stones used in the Bible to build altars. Have kids use crayons to draw pictures of people or things people sometimes put before God. When they're done coloring, let kids arrange their pictures in a circle on the floor.

Say: **People put lots of different things first in their lives, but there is only one God. He deserves to be first! He proved he's God when he sent fire from heaven to burn up the altar Elijah made.** Invite kids to turn over their paper and draw fire on the blank side.

Say: **God is more powerful than anyone or anything. He's the one true God.**

# One True God

## Game

**SUPPLIES**

scraps of red, yellow, and orange paper; brown squares of paper; tape; blindfolds

**B**efore children arrive, tape the brown squares of paper to a wall to resemble an altar. You'll need two altars several feet apart. Also place rolled-up pieces of tape on the backs of red, yellow, and orange scraps of paper.

Say: **Elijah knew that only God was the real God and that Baal wouldn't be able to beat him in a contest. Let's have a contest to see how well we can make fires.**

Help kids form two teams, and blindfold everyone on just one of the teams. Give every child on both teams a scrap of red, yellow, or orange paper with a piece of tape on the back—these paper scraps will be flames. The two teams will see who can get the most flames on their altar.

When the game starts, spin the kids on the blindfolded team around a few times and face them in the wrong direction so they're not headed toward the altar. Let the kids who can see take turns going up and placing their flames on their altar. After everyone has had a turn, remove blindfolds and have kids see how they did.

Ask:

- *Why was one team so much better than the other team?*
- *Why is God better than anything else?*

Play the game again, this time letting all the kids see so they can place their flames on the altar. Each time a child places a flame, have him or her say, "The Lord is the one true God!"

# Eating With God

## Snack

**SUPPLIES**

paper plates, graham crackers, mini marshmallows, hot fudge sauce, antibacterial gel (optional)

*ALLERGY ALERT!*
See page 5

**S**ay: **In Bible times, people built altars to worship God. They would bring God gifts and pray. If they brought food, they would either burn it on the altar or eat it near the altar while they prayed. Elijah asked God to burn up his offering with fire from heaven. Let's build altars like Elijah did and thank God for things he's done.**

Have kids clean their hands, and let kids build altars using graham cracker squares for the base, mini marshmallows for bricks, and hot fudge sauce for mortar. While they work, encourage kids to think of things God has done for them and thank him for those things. When kids finish building their altars, thank God for providing the snack, and then let kids eat and enjoy.

# The Lord, He Is God

## Song

**SUPPLIES**

**S**ay: **Let's sing a song to remind us the Lord is God—the only real God.** Teach preschoolers the following words and motions to the tune of "Row, Row, Row Your Boat."

Sing:

**The Lord, he is God.** *(point up)*

**Yes, the Lord is God.** *(raise hands above head and wiggle hands)*

**He set fire to water and stone.** *(slowly bring hands down in front while wiggling fingers)*

**He proved that he is God.** *(raise hands high and wiggle hands)*

# Baal Will Fail

## Action Play

SUPPLIES

**R**ead your preschoolers the following rhyme about Elijah and the prophets of Baal, having them follow along as you do the actions in parentheses while you read each line.

Rhyme:

**Elijah prayed to the one true God.** *(point up)*

**King Ahab prayed to Baal.** *(shake finger back and forth in front)*

**Elijah said, "Baal will fail,** *(sweep hands away, palms down)*

**And my God will prevail."** *(place fists on hips and stand tall)*

**King Ahab's prophets called on Baal.** *(cup hands around mouth)*

**Sure he would never fail.** *(sweep hands away, palms down)*

**They danced and shouted, never doubted.** *(skip in place)*

**But all to no avail.** *(shake head back and forth)*

**That Baal, he didn't say a word.** *(place index finger over lips)*

**His voice they didn't hear.** *(cup hands over ears)*

**Shocked at what he saw and heard,** *(raise eyebrows and place hands on cheeks)*

**Elijah said, "Come here."** *(wave to self)*

**He made an altar there and prayed.** *(pound fists on top of each other; then make praying hands)*

**The Lord God won the day.** *(place fists on hips and stand tall)*

**The people knelt and worshipped God;** *(bow at the waist)*

**From Baal they turned away.** *(spin around)*

**SUPPLIES**

# You're My God

## Prayer

**L**ead preschoolers in this responsive prayer. Pray the bold words aloud, and invite kids to say the response with you and do the motions.

Pray:

**Oh, Lord, you're my God.** *(raise one fist in the air)*

**Yes, you're my God.** *(thrust finger toward heaven)*

**You answered Elijah's prayer.** *(make praying hands)*

**Yes, you're my God.** *(thrust finger toward heaven)*

**You sent fire from heaven.** *(slowly bring hands down in front while wiggling fingers)*

**Yes, you're my God.** *(thrust finger toward heaven)*

**You showed you're the only God.** *(shake finger back and forth)*

**Yes, you're my God.** *(thrust finger toward heaven)*

**Oh, Lord, you're my God.** *(raise one fist in the air)*

**Yes, you're my God.** *(thrust finger toward heaven)*

**In Jesus' name, amen.**

# God Tells Jonah to Obey

## Jonah 1:1–3:10

## Obey God: Listen and Do

### Bible Experience

 **SUPPLIES**

Bible, paper towels soaked in tuna-fish oil and stored in a resealable plastic bag, large bedsheet, large blocks, spray bottle of water

 ALLERGY ALERT! See page 5

**B**efore children arrive, drape a bedsheet over a table and leave two ends open.

Have children gather and sit with you in a circle. Open your Bible to Jonah 1, and show children the words. Tell them the Bible is God's special book.

Say: **The Bible says God told Jonah to obey. To *obey* means to listen *and* do. When we obey God we listen to him *and* do what he says.**

**God told Jonah to go to a town called Nineveh. Jonah didn't obey. He listened, but he didn't do what God said. Instead Jonah ran the other way.** Have children stand and run in place. **When Jonah was done running, he got on a boat.** Instruct children to help place blocks in a boat shape large enough for everyone to fit in. Then have everyone sit in the boat. **Thank you for being good helpers and obeying. *Obeying* means listening and doing, and you listened and did what I asked. You obeyed.**

Ask:

- *What are some things your moms and dads ask you to do?*

Say: **When you listen and then do what your parents ask, that means you're obeying your parents. God wants us to obey our parents and obey him.**

**Jonah wasn't obeying God. He got in the boat and went to sleep.** Have children pretend to sleep. **While he slept, the wind started to blow.** Have children blow with their mouths to create wind. **Big waves started to crash on the boat as it rocked in the wind.** Have children rock in the boat while making slow, loud clapping noises for waves. Spray them gently with some water from the spray bottle.

Ask:

- *Tell about a storm you've seen.*
- *What do you do when you're scared?*

Say: **The other people on the boat woke Jonah up. They asked Jonah to pray to his God to make the storm stop. Jonah knew the storm came because he hadn't obeyed God. And he still wasn't ready to obey. Instead he asked the other people to throw him into the water. The people didn't want to do it, but they really wanted the storm to stop. So Jonah went into the water with a loud splash.** Spray water again.

**After Jonah went into the water, a very big fish came and swallowed him up with a big gulp.** Make a loud gulping sound. Then let children all make gulping noises. **Jonah stayed in that fish for three days. He started to smell like a stinky fish.** Hold the resealable plastic bag, and let children smell the paper towels dipped in tuna-fish oil. Be aware that tuna commonly triggers fish allergies, so be sure you don't have any kids who are allergic to fish before you do this activity.

Ask:

- *What things happen to you when you don't obey your mom and dad?*

Say: **While he was inside the fish, Jonah prayed to God and said, "God, I'll obey you. I'll listen and do."** As a group, have children say, "God, I'll obey you. I'll listen and do."

Ask:

- *Why is obeying a good thing to do?*

Say: **God heard Jonah's prayer and had the fish spit Jonah out on dry land.**

**Let's pretend we're going inside a big fish the way Jonah did.** Let children take turns going under the bedsheet-covered table. When they get in, have them count to three to represent three days inside the big fish. When they come out, have them say, "God, I'll obey you. I'll listen and do."

**After the fish spit Jonah out, Jonah obeyed God. He went to Nineveh and told the people there to stop doing bad things and to believe in God and only do good things. And the people in Nineveh obeyed—they listened to Jonah and did what he said.**

Ask:

- *What are some good things you can do?*
- *Where are some places you could go to tell people about God?*

# In and Out of a Fish

## Craft

**SUPPLIES**

for each child: 1 cardboard tube, a large fish shape cut out of 9 x 12-inch sheets of construction paper, and a strip of poster board slightly longer than the fish and a bit narrower than the cardboard tube; tape; crayons or washable markers

**G**ive each child a cardboard tube, a fish shape, and a strip of poster board. Set out crayons or markers, and let children decorate the paper fish. When they're done, help children draw a person on the end of their poster board strip. This will be "Jonah."

Help children each tape the cardboard tube onto the back of their fish; then let children put the poster-board strip into the cardboard tube with the drawing of Jonah facing forward nearest the fish's mouth. Children can then push the strip in and out of the tube to look like the fish is swallowing Jonah and then spitting him out. When children let Jonah out of the fish, have them say, "I will obey. I will listen to God."

# Can You Obey?

## Game

**SUPPLIES**

**S**ay: **God wants us to obey—he wants us to obey our parents and obey him. To *obey* means to listen to and do what someone says. Let's try to obey right now.** Give children actions to follow. Start with easy, one-step directions, such as "jump up and down," "touch your head," or "flap your arms."

**Now let's try something a little harder.** Give a two-step direction, such as "jump and shake your head" or "bend and twist."

**Let's see if anyone can listen and do this.** Give a set of directions that will be too hard to follow, such as "turn around, touch your head, touch your foot, bend your knee, and wiggle your nose."

Ask:

- *Why was it so hard to obey at the end?*
- *When is it hardest for you to obey?*

Say: **Sometimes it's really hard to obey. Even big people can have a hard time obeying sometimes. But we can always keep trying.**

If you have time, you can invite willing children to pick an action for others to try to obey.

# Obey

## Snack

**SUPPLIES**

1 teddy graham cracker or gummy bear per child, hot-dog buns cut in half the short way, cream cheese colored with blue food coloring, paper plates, plastic spoons, antibacterial gel (optional)

*ALLERGY ALERT!*
*See page 5*

**S**ay: **When Jonah was inside the big fish, he prayed to God and chose to obey him. Let's have a snack to remind us that we can pray to God just as Jonah did—and we can choose to obey him, too.**

Have children clean their hands before preparing their snacks. Invite a willing child to pray, asking God to help us obey.

Give each child a plastic spoon and a spoonful of blue cream cheese on a plate. Let children spread the cream cheese around with the plastic spoon to resemble waves. Give children each half a hot-dog bun and a teddy graham cracker, and let them put the teddy inside the bun to remind them of Jonah in the big fish. Let children dip their buns into the cream cheese and eat and enjoy.

As kids eat, say: **When Jonah was swallowed by a big fish, he found out it's not good to disobey God.** Have kids share about times they learned it's not good to disobey.

# Jonah Chose to Follow

## Song

**SUPPLIES**

**S**ay: **Let's sing a song about Jonah obeying God.** Teach preschoolers the following words and motions to the tune of "B-I-N-G-O."

Sing:

**God wanted Jonah to obey,**

**But Jonah wouldn't follow.**

**No, no, no, no, no.** *(shake head no)*

**No, no, no, no, no.** *(shake head no)*

**No, no, no, no, no.** *(shake head no)*

**And Jonah wouldn't follow.**

**Then Jonah had a great big storm,**

**Was swallowed by a fish.**

**Gulp, gulp, gulp, gulp, gulp.** *(press wrists together and move hands to look like a mouth opening and closing)*

**Gulp, gulp, gulp, gulp, gulp.** *(press wrists together and move hands to look like a mouth opening and closing)*

**Gulp, gulp, gulp, gulp, gulp.** *(press wrists together and move hands to look like a mouth opening and closing)*

**He prayed inside a fish.**

**Then Jonah listened to our God,**

**And Jonah chose to follow.**

**Yes, yes, yes, yes, yes.** *(shake head yes)*

**Yes, yes, yes, yes, yes.** *(shake head yes)*

**Yes, yes, yes, yes, yes.** *(shake head yes)*

**And Jonah chose to follow.**

# Jonah Gets Out of His Mess

## Action Play

**R**ead preschoolers the following rhyme about Jonah, having them follow along as you do the actions in parentheses while you read each line.

Rhyme:

**God told Jonah to go, go, go.** *(walk in place)*

**Jonah told God, "No, no, no."** *(shake head no)*

**Jonah ran the other way.** *(run in place)*

**He climbed into a boat to stay.** *(make climbing motions)*

**A big storm came with a great big "whoosh!"** *(make blowing sounds and wave arms)*

**The sailors gave Jonah a great big push.** *(push arms out in front)*

**Jonah fell into a fish's belly.** *(put hands on belly)*

**Inside the fish was pretty smelly.** *(hold nose)*

**Jonah was sorry and started to pray.** *(make praying hands)*

**He wanted to go a different way.** *(walk in place)*

**This time Jonah said, "Yes, yes, yes."** *(shake head yes)*

**And Jonah was happily out of his mess.** *(turn around and wave arms joyfully)*

# Helping Prayers

## Prayer

SUPPLIES

bedsheet, soft doll or stuffed figure

**H**ave children gather around a bedsheet and hold its edges. Place a doll in the middle to represent Jonah. Let children gently shake the sheet to show how the storm rocked Jonah's boat. Then stop the kids' shaking, and choose a child.

Say: [Name of child], **talk to God and tell him something he can help you do for someone.** Allow time for the child to pray.

Have kids shake the sheet again, and pick a different child to pray. Let everyone have a turn praying to God. If you have more than eight children, have two children pray before shaking the sheet again. After everyone has had a turn, close the time with the following prayer.

Pray:

**Dear God, thank you for helping us obey you and do good things for people. In Jesus' name, amen.**

# Jesus Is Born

## Luke 2:8-20

## Exciting News!

### Bible Experience

SUPPLIES

Bible

**H**ave children sit in a circle with you. Open your Bible to Luke 2, and show children the words. Tell them the Bible is God's special book.

Say: **The Bible tells about shepherds who were in their fields one night watching their sheep. Shepherds are people who take care of sheep.** Let children make sheep noises. **Then something scared the shepherds.** Have kids make scared faces.

Ask:

- *What's something that scares you?*
- *What helps you not be afraid?*

Say: **What scared the shepherds was an angel. It appeared to them very suddenly with a bright light all around. But the angel said, "Don't be afraid! I bring you good news that will bring great joy to all people. The Savior—yes, the Messiah, the Lord—has been born today in Bethlehem, the city of David! You will find a baby wrapped snugly in strips of cloth lying in a manger." This was really good news! Then even more angels appeared and they all said, "Glory to God."** Have children stand up and pretend they're angels, holding up their arms and shouting "Glory to God!" several times.

**The angels went back to heaven, and the shepherds wanted to go see the baby.** Lead children in walking to the left, walking to the right, climbing up a hill, moving slowly, moving quickly, and then sitting down. **When they got to the village, they found Mary—the baby's mother—Joseph, and a baby lying in a manger, just as the angel said. The baby's name was Jesus. The shepherds were so excited!** Have children demonstrate how they look or what they do when they're excited.

Ask:

- *What's something that's really exciting for you?*
- *Why is hearing that Jesus is born so exciting?*

Say: **The shepherds ran off to tell other people about Jesus.** Have kids run in place. **When the shepherds told other people that Jesus was born, the people were amazed.** Have kids tell each other "Jesus is born," and have children respond with looks of amazement.

Ask:

- *Who are some people you like to share exciting news with?*

Say: **The shepherds went back to their fields and continued to praise God for baby Jesus' birth.** Have kids give high fives in praise to God.

# My Hand Holds Jesus

## Craft

**SUPPLIES**

paper, pen, 2-inch ovals cut out of paper or craft foam, washable markers, glue, 1 square of toilet tissue per child, short pieces of yellow yarn, washable brown tempera paint, large paintbrushes, washable markers, paper towels, smocks (optional)

**S**ay: **Let's make a craft to remember that Jesus was born in a manger.**

Distribute sheets of paper. Set out brown tempera paint, paintbrushes, and paper towels. You may want to put a smock on each child. Help children paint the palm and fingers of one hand (no thumbs). Then help kids make a handprint with fingers spread and pointing toward the bottom of the paper to resemble a manger. Help children wash off their hands, and then write children's names on their pages. Give children each an oval shape, and let them draw a face at one end of it with a marker. Help children wrap their oval shapes with toilet tissue, leaving the face uncovered. Help children glue yellow yarn pieces onto the palm part of their handprint to look like hay. Finally, have kids glue the swaddled baby onto the manger.

Say: **Jesus may have had a small start. But he was the most important person who ever lived!**

**Teacher TIP**

You could use a large stamp pad and washable brown ink instead of paint.

# Let's Go to Bethlehem

## Game

**SUPPLIES**

gift bags, pictures of baby Jesus, pictures of sheep, music player and upbeat preschool-friendly praise music

**S**ay: **Let's play a game about the shepherds who found baby Jesus. Some people will be shepherds and the rest of us will be their sheep.** Divide children into groups of five, and appoint one Shepherd for each group. Place a picture of Jesus and two or three pictures of sheep into a gift bag (one bag for each group). Play music, and have children follow their Shepherd wherever he or she takes them, doing whatever the Shepherd does. If needed, prompt the Shepherds to do actions like hopping, clapping hands, or flying like an airplane.

Occasionally stop the music, and say: **Jesus is born!** Have Shepherds reach into their bags—without looking—and pull out a picture to see if they found baby Jesus. If they get the picture of baby Jesus, that group will say, "Jesus is born!" If they get the picture of the sheep, the group will say, "We're still looking for Jesus." Restart the music and play the game again, choosing a new Shepherd for each group.

Say: **The shepherds kept searching until they found Jesus because they knew how special he was. We can look for Jesus, too.**

# Jesus in a Manger

## Snack

**SUPPLIES**

shredded wheat cereal, graham crackers, teddy graham crackers, paper plates, antibacterial gel (optional)

ALLERGY ALERT!
See page 5

**S**ay: **The Bible tells us Jesus was born in a manger. A manger is a box filled with hay for animals to eat. Let's make a manger snack to remember Jesus' birth.**

Have children clean their hands before they prepare their snacks. Give children each a graham cracker on a plate. Let them crush a couple of shredded wheat biscuits in their hands onto a graham cracker. Give each child a teddy graham to place in the middle. Invite children to pray, thanking God for sending his son, Jesus.

While children eat, ask the following questions.

Ask:

- *Do you think a manger is a good place for a baby to sleep? Why or why not?*
- *If you could make baby Jesus any bed, what would it look like?*

# Baby Jesus, We Love You

## Song

**SUPPLIES**

**S**ay: **Let's sing a song about baby Jesus.** Teach preschoolers the following words and motions to the tune of "Are You Sleeping?"

Sing:

**Baby Jesus, baby Jesus,** *(rock baby in arms)*

**We love you, we love you.** *(hug self)*

**Let's tell the world about you,** *(cup hands to mouth)*

**Tell the world about you.** *(cup hands to mouth)*

**We love you, we love you.** *(hug self)*

*(Repeat two or three times.)*

# Looking for Baby Jesus

## Action Play

**SUPPLIES**

**R**ead your preschoolers the following rhyme about baby Jesus, having them follow along as you do the actions in parentheses while you read each line.

Rhyme:

**Let's look for baby Jesus.** *(shade eyes with hands and look around)*

**Is he in the sky?** *(shade eyes with hands and look up)*

**Is he lying way down low,** *(crouch down low to the floor)*

**Or is he way up high?** *(stand on tiptoes)*

**I see baby Jesus.** *(point in front)*

**Sleeping in the hay.** *(lay head on hands)*

**I see Jesus in my heart,** *(point to heart)*

**Every night and day.** *(cross hands over heart)*

# I Love You More

## Prayer

**SUPPLIES**

cotton balls

**H**ave kids gather and sit in a circle with you.

Say: **In the Bible, the sheep were very important to the shepherds. The shepherds cared very much for their sheep. But when the shepherds met baby Jesus, they loved him far more than they loved their sheep. It's important that we love Jesus more than anything or anyone in *our* lives.** Give each child a cotton ball as a reminder of the sheep. Have children think of something they love that's important to them. Invite children to pray, finishing the statement "Jesus, I love you more than…" As children pray, have them place their cotton balls on the floor.

After everyone has had a turn, close with the following prayer.

Pray:

**Thank you, God, for sending your son, Jesus, as a baby. Help us always give him first place in our lives. In Jesus' name, amen.**

# Jesus Heals a Man

## John 5:2-9

## Stand Up and Walk

### Bible Experience

**SUPPLIES**

Bible

**H**ave children sit in a circle with you. Open your Bible to John 5, and show children the words. Tell them the Bible is God's special book.

Say: **The Bible says Jesus once healed a man who had been sick for 38 years.**

Ask:

- *What's the longest time you've been sick?*
- *What's it like when you're sick?*

Say: **Thirty-eight years is a long time to be sick. And this man was sick in a way that he wasn't able to walk. Let's see what it's like to not be able to move.** Have kids stand in front of you and strike a pose. Tell them not to move until you finish counting. Count slowly to 38.

**Whew! Okay, everyone, shake out your arms and legs and have a seat.**

Ask:

- *What was the hardest part about not being able to move?*
- *What are some things that would be difficult to do if you couldn't move?*

Say: **This man wanted to be healed. The way for him to be healed was to be the first one into the pool of Bethesda. To do that, he needed help getting there. And there was no one there to help him.**

Ask:

- *When was a time you needed help doing something?*
- *What was it like when someone helped you?*
- *Tell about a time you helped someone else.*

Say: **Then Jesus came by. Jesus saw the man and asked him if he wanted to be healed.**

Ask:

- *What's something you want that you can tell Jesus about?*

Say: **The man said he did want to be healed, but he couldn't get to the pool fast enough. So Jesus told him, "Stand up, pick up your mat, and walk!" Instantly the man was healed. He rolled up his sleeping mat and walked.**

Have kids stand up and pretend to roll up a mat. Lead kids around the room saying, "Jesus healed the man. Hallelujah!"

# Take Up Your Mat

## Craft

**SUPPLIES**

1 large sheet of paper per child, washable markers

**L**ay out a large sheet of paper for each child, and set out markers. Have kids create their own mats by drawing on the paper with the markers. When kids have finished making their mats, have them lie on them.

Remind kids how the man Jesus healed had to lie on his mat because he couldn't walk on his own.

Ask:

- *Why do you think Jesus had to tell the man to pick up his mat and walk?*
- *What do you think it was like for the man to walk after not walking for such a long time?*

Say: **When Jesus healed the man by the pool, the man had to do something to show he was healed. Jesus still heals and helps us today. Sometimes he also tells us to do something that shows what he has done for us. When he does that, we need to obey.**

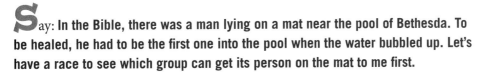

# Time to Move

# Game

SUPPLIES

1 bath-size towel for every 3 kids, clear glass of water, straw

**S**ay: **In the Bible, there was a man lying on a mat near the pool of Bethesda. To be healed, he had to be the first one into the pool when the water bubbled up. Let's have a race to see which group can get its person on the mat to me first.**

Help kids form trios, and give each group a towel. Have the trios stand on the other side of the room facing you. Kids will take turns sitting on the towel and being pulled by the other two kids. Tell the kids sitting on the towels to hold on tight so they don't flip off. If a child does fall off the towel, have the child get back on and continue. Have kids start pulling when they see you blow bubbles into the glass of water with the straw.

Repeat two more times so each child gets a turn on the mat.

Ask:

- *What was this game like for you?*
- *What's it like when you lose a race?*

Say: **When Jesus came along and talked to the man, the man was discouraged that he couldn't get to the pool quick enough.**

Ask:

- *Tell about a time you've been discouraged because you couldn't do something.*
- *How could you encourage someone who's discouraged?*

# Fruit Mats

## Snack

**S**ay: **Jesus healed a man who had been sick for a very long time. Jesus asked the man if he wanted to get well. Of course the man said yes! So Jesus told him to stand up, pick up his mat, and walk. The man did just what Jesus told him to, and Jesus healed him. Let's make a snack that reminds us that Jesus can heal us, too.**

Have kids clean their hands. Give each child four sections of a Fruit by the Foot, and have kids place two sections next to each other on a paper plate. Help kids "weave" the other two sections into the first two to form a mat.

Have kids roll up their fruit mats and march around the room, cheering as they go. Then have them pray to thank God for their snack, and let them eat and enjoy.

# Healed From Head to Toe

## Song

SUPPLIES

**S**ay: **Let's sing a song about how Jesus healed the sick man.** Teach preschoolers the following words and motions to the tune of "London Bridge Is Falling Down."

Sing:

**Jesus healed from head to toe,** *(point up; then touch top of head, and then touch toes)*

**Head to toe;** *(touch top of head; then toes)*

**Head to toe.** *(touch top of head; then toes)*

**Jesus healed from head to toe,** *(point up; then touch top of head, and then touch toes)*

**That's my Jesus!** *(point up)*

# Get Me to the Pool

## Action Play

SUPPLIES

**R**ead your preschoolers the following rhyme about Jesus healing the man who couldn't walk. Have them follow along as you do the actions in parentheses while you read each line.

Rhyme:

**A man was sick for many years.** *(slump shoulders)*

**Each day he'd say through his tears,** *(rub eyes with fists)*

**"Will someone take me to the pool today?"** *(clasp hands in front as if pleading)*

**The crowds of people kept away.** *(put palms out, arms extended)*

**Jesus was walking by that place.** *(walk in place)*

**And when he looked into the man's face,** *(shade eyes with hands)*

**Jesus asked him, "Do you want to get well?"** *(hold hands out to side, palms up)*

**The man said, "Yes, that would be swell!"** *(nod head)*

**Jesus said, "Stand up! Be well!"** *(stand up tall)*

**The man got up, picked up his mat,** *(pretend to pick up mat from floor)*

**And he could walk! Imagine that!** *(walk in place; then raise eyebrows and place hands on cheeks in amazement)*

# Jesus Answers

## Prayer

**G**ive each child a piece of paper and crayons. Have children each draw a picture of someone they know who needs to be healed by Jesus. Help them each write the name of the person on their paper.

Say: **Jesus heals people, just like he healed the man next to the pool. Let's ask Jesus to heal the people we drew pictures of.**

Have kids form a circle with you. Have children hold their drawings so everyone else can see them. As you pray the following prayer, have kids each say the name of the person they're praying for.

Pray:

**Dear Jesus, thank you for healing the man by the pool who had been sick for a very long time. We pray that you would also heal** [have each child speak the name of the person]. **Thank you, Jesus, for hearing our prayers. We love you and trust you. In your name we pray, amen.**

# Jesus Feeds More Than 5,000 People

## John 6:1-14

## Share What You Have

### Bible Experience

**SUPPLIES**

Bible, confetti, large clear container, large opaque bowl

**H**ave kids stand in a circle with you. Open your Bible to John 6, and show kids the words. Tell them the Bible is God's special book.

Say: **The Bible tells about a time Jesus was able to feed a huge crowd of people with just a small amount of food. Jesus had gone up on a hill to be with his disciples.** Lead kids around the room in a quick game of Follow the Leader. End by forming the group into a circle; then have everyone sit down. **A large crowd of people—more than 5,000—had followed Jesus and his disciples because they had seen Jesus heal so many people. It was close to mealtime, and when Jesus and the disciples saw all the people coming, they wondered how they'd all have enough to eat.**

Ask:

- *What could you do if you had to feed a lot of people?*

Say: **One of the disciples told Jesus about a boy in the crowd who was willing to share his lunch of five loaves of bread and two fishes.**

Ask:

- *What's your favorite food to pack for a lunch when you're not eating at home?*
- *Tell about a time you shared with someone.*

Say: **Jesus had all the people sit down, gave thanks for the bread and fish, and shared it with everyone. The people were able to eat as much as they wanted until they were full.** Have kids pretend to eat a meal as you continue. **The disciples gathered up all the leftovers—enough to fill 12 baskets!** Have kids walk around the room pretending to fill baskets with food. After about a minute, gather kids back together and have them sit down. **It was a miracle!**

**Let's see what it might've been like when the bread and fish were multiplied.** Set out an empty clear container and an opaque bowl full of confetti. Have one child come up and count out five pieces of confetti—representing the loaves—and place them in the clear container. Have another child come up and count out two pieces of confetti—representing the fish—and place them in the clear container as well. Hold up the container so all the kids can see it.

**Now let's see what happened when Jesus multiplied the food.** Have the rest of the kids come up and each place a handful of confetti in with the other seven pieces. Continue until all the confetti is transferred from the opaque bowl to the clear container. Hold up the clear container again.

**Look at how much our confetti multiplied! We started out with just a few pieces and ended up with so much more. Jesus did that with the bread and fish, but he didn't have a bowl to pull the extra from. What Jesus did was a miracle. And it all started with one boy who was willing to share his lunch.**

Ask:

- *When has something good happened because you shared with someone?*
- *What are some things besides food you could share with others?*

# Jesus Provides

## Craft

**SUPPLIES**

1 copy per child of the "Food Basket" handout (at the end of this chapter), magazines with pictures of food, several pairs of scissors, glue sticks, crayons

**S**ay: **Let's make something to remind us that Jesus can use us to provide for the needs of others.**

Give each child a copy of the "Food Basket" handout, and set out magazines, scissors, glue sticks, and crayons. Let kids color the basket any way they choose, and then help kids cut out pictures of food they like and glue the pictures to their handouts.

Ask:

- *How many people do you think the food in your picture could feed?*
- *What could you do if you had to feed everyone in your neighborhood with only the food in your picture?*

Say: **Jesus fed more than 5,000 people with the five loaves of bread and two fishes the boy gave him.**

Ask:

- *What can you do to help feed hungry people today?*
- *What are other things you can do to help provide for other people's needs?*

# Time to Share

## Game

**SUPPLIES**

10 stickers per child

**G**ive each child 10 stickers. Say: **In the Bible, we learned about a boy who shared his food with Jesus who then was able to miraculously feed more than 5,000 people. Today we're going to practice sharing. You have 10 stickers. When I say "go," you'll try to share all your stickers as quickly as possible by sticking them to 10 different people. Ready? Go!**

Allow time for kids to all share their stickers. Then have kids count how many stickers they ended up with. Help kids even things out if some kids got a lot of stickers and some didn't get as many.

Ask:

- *Why is it important to be fair when you share with others?*
- *What are some things people have shared with you? How have those things helped you?*

Say: **It's always important to share. We may have something that someone else needs, and they may have something we need. If we work together to share, we both get what we need. In the Bible, the people needed food. A boy was willing to share and everyone was able to eat. Jesus can use what we share to help other people.**

# Jesus Makes It More

## Snack

**SUPPLIES**

pretzel sticks, cheese crackers, Chex cereal, teddy bear graham crackers, small resealable plastic bags, large mixing bowl, antibacterial gel (optional)

*ALLERGY ALERT!*
See page 5

**B**efore children arrive, put individual ingredients into separate resealable plastic bags. Make enough bags so each child will have a bag of a single ingredient.

Have kids get into four groups. Give each group a different snack ingredient, allowing each child in each group to have his or her own bag. Instruct kids not to eat yet.

Say: **The boy who shared his lunch only brought a few things to eat. But when he gave those things to Jesus, it became enough to feed thousands of people!**

**Let's have a snack that reminds us Jesus can take the little bit we give him and make it into a lot.**

Have children clean their hands and then take turns dumping the contents of their bags into a large bowl. After all the kids have added their ingredients to the bowl, mix the ingredients. Put snack portions of the mix back into the bags and give one bag to each child. Let kids eat and enjoy.

Say: **When we're willing to share what we have, Jesus can make it into more.** On the count of three, have kids shout, "Thank you, Jesus!"

# Sharing, Sharing

## Song

**SUPPLIES**

**S**ay: **In the Bible, the little boy shared his lunch. Let's sing a song that reminds us to share.** Teach preschoolers the following words to the tune of "Bicycle Built for Two." Have kids form pairs and hold hands facing each other. Have them go up and down (like a seesaw) as they sing.

Sing:

**Sharing, sharing,**

**That's what we need to do.**

**I love sharing**

**All of my things with you.**

**I may not have lots to give you**

**But share is what I will do.**

**Because I care, I'm gonna share**

**Every one of my things with you.**

# Bread and Fish for All

## Action Play

**SUPPLIES**

**R**ead preschoolers the following rhyme about Jesus feeding the 5,000, having them follow along as you do the actions in parentheses while you read each line.

Rhyme:

**Five loaves of bread,** *(hold up five fingers)*

**Two little fish,** *(hold up two fingers)*

**A whole lot of people,** *(spread arms out wide)*

**And one big wish.** *(clasp hands in front)*

**A tiny lunch** *(hold up index finger and thumb slightly apart)*

**To feed a crowd** *(bring hand to mouth as if eating)*

**Whose hungry stomachs** *(put hands on stomach)*

**Were growling loud.** *(put hands up and spread fingers like bear claws)*

**It was past time to eat.** *(put hands on stomach and shake head no)*

**He broke fish and bread.** *(make a breaking motion with hands)*

**The people sat down.** *(squat to the floor)*

**"Thanks to God," he said.** *(make praying hands)*

**He passed out the fish.** *(put one hand out in front, palm up)*

**He passed out the bread.** *(put second hand out in front, palm up)*

**There was more than enough.** *(spread arms out wide)*

**All the people were fed.** *(rub stomach with hands)*

**Twelve baskets left over,** *(make a circle with arms in front)*

**The crowd satisfied,** *(put hands on stomach)*

**"Oh wow, what a miracle!"** *(raise eyebrows and place hands on cheeks)*

**"Praise to God," they cried.** *(raise arms above head and wiggle hands)*

# Lunchbox Prayer

## Prayer

**H**ave kids sit in a circle with you.

Say: **The boy who shared his lunch didn't know what Jesus was going to do with it. He didn't know how much of his lunch he would still get to eat. But he was still willing to share.**

Ask:

- *What's one thing you have trouble sharing?*
- *What good things can happen when you share those items?*

Say: **Let's pray and tell Jesus we're willing to share even those things that are hard to share. And let's ask Jesus to use the things we share to help others.**

Pass an empty lunchbox around the circle. When a child receives the lunchbox, it's his or her turn to pray. Have children tell Jesus they're willing to share even the thing they mentioned is hard to share. After everyone has prayed, close the time with the following prayer.

Pray:

**Dear Jesus, thank you for teaching us to share. Thank you for showing us you can do good things when we share. And thank you for helping us share, even when it's hard. In your name we pray, amen.**

# Food Basket

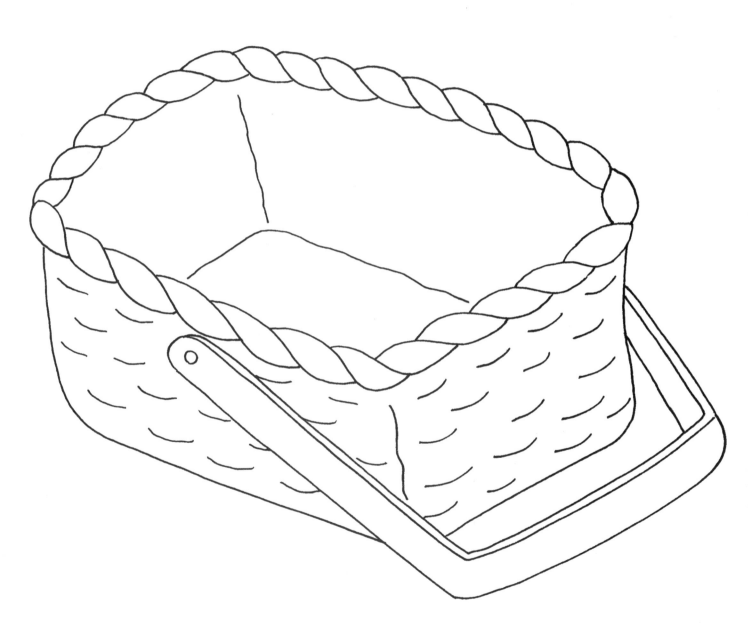

# The Miraculous Catch of Fish

## John 21:1-13

## So Many Fish!

### Bible Experience

**SUPPLIES**

Bible, masking tape

**B**efore kids arrive, use masking tape to create a boat shape on the floor that's large enough for everyone to sit inside later on.

Have children sit in a circle on the floor with you. Open your Bible to John 21, and show kids the words. Tell them the Bible is God's special book.

Say: **The Bible tells about a time Jesus came to his disciples after he died and rose from the grave. The disciples were Jesus' friends. Some of the disciples had decided to go fishing.** Have kids sit in the boat shape and pretend to hold fishing poles. Have them all pretend to cast their fishing lines off the left side of the boat.

**The disciples weren't able to catch anything all night. In the morning while they were still on the boat, Jesus appeared on the beach and told them to try fishing from the right-hand side of the boat.** Have kids raise their right hands. **The disciples didn't recognize Jesus, but they went ahead and did what he told them to do.** Have all the kids pretend to cast their lines off the right-hand side of the boat. **When they did, they caught so many fish they couldn't pull the fish into the boat!** Pretend you caught a fish on your line that's too heavy for you. Have the children come around you to help try pulling the fish into the boat. Pretend that, even with all their help, you just can't get the fish in the boat.

**That's when John—one of the disciples—realized the man on the beach was Jesus. John told Peter the man was Jesus. Peter was so excited Jesus was there that he jumped into the water and swam to shore.** Have three children step out of the boat shape and pretend to swim. **The other disciples came to shore in the boat, pulling all the fish with them.** Have the kids who are still in the boat pretend to row with a heavy net full of fish.

**When the disciples got to the beach, Jesus had already made a fire. He cooked fish for them and had bread as well. So the disciples got to have a special breakfast with Jesus.** Have all the kids step out of the boat shape and sit in a circle with you on the floor. Lead them in pretending there's a fire in the center of your circle and you're all eating breakfast.

Ask:

- *When is a time you got to have a special breakfast with someone?*
- *What do you think about Jesus giving his friends all those fish?*
- *What do you think about Jesus cooking breakfast for his special friends?*

Say: **The disciples recognized Jesus after he helped them catch all those fish.**

# Net Full of Fish

## Craft

**SUPPLIES**

1 hairnet per child, 1-foot lengths of yarn, small fish shapes cut out of poster board, crayons

**S**ay: **When the disciples went fishing, they used nets to catch their fish. Let's make a net full of fish to remind us of the miracle Jesus performed.**

Give each child several poster-board fish. Set out crayons, and have kids color their fish in any way they choose. When they're done, have children place all their fish to their right. Then place a hairnet to each child's left.

**After the disciples told Jesus they hadn't caught any fish, he told them to cast their net on the right-hand side of the boat and they *would* catch fish.** Have kids raise their right hands, and then have them move their nets from their left sides to their right sides next to their fish. Have kids place their fish inside their hairnets. Help them each close up the opening in their hairnet and tie it with yarn.

**Jesus helped his friends do something that they were having a hard time doing. They couldn't catch fish, so Jesus helped them catch a lot of fish in their nets.**

Ask:

- *When have you had a hard time doing something?*
- *When has someone helped you do something you couldn't do on your own?*
- *What is a way you could help someone who is having a hard time?*

Say: **Jesus always has the right answer and knows just what to do!**

# Fish Bounce

## Game

**SUPPLIES**

large bedsheet, 10 inflated balloons with a fish drawn on each one

*BALLOON WARNING!*
See page 5

**S**ay: **When the disciples caught all the fish in their net, they had to work together to get the fish into the boat. Let's play a game to see what it's like working together to get something done.**

Spread a bedsheet on the floor. Have kids gather around the sheet and each hold an edge, lifting the sheet off the floor. Tell them the sheet is their net. Toss one balloon onto the sheet. The balloon is the fish. Have kids move the sheet up and down like waves in the water. Tell them to try keeping the fish on the net. As kids bounce the balloon on the sheet, occasionally add a balloon. The more balloons you add, the harder it'll get.

Keep going until you've tossed all the balloons onto the sheet. It's okay if some bounce off—just pick them up and toss them back on. After all the fish have gone into the net, have kids set the sheet down and sit down around it.

Ask:

- *What was it like trying to keep the balloons on the sheet?*
- *Why was it important to have everyone work together to keep the balloons on the sheet?*
- *What are some ways you can work together with someone in your family to help get something done?*

Say: **Jesus loves it when we work together for him.**

# Snack Catch

**SUPPLIES**

fish crackers, small disposable cups, 2 large opaque bowls or plastic tubs, antibacterial gel (optional)

**ALLERGY ALERT!**
See page 5

## Snack

**S**et two bowls up high enough that kids can reach in but can't see what's in them. Fill the bowl on the right full of fish crackers. Leave the bowl on the left empty. Have kids clean their hands, and then have kids stand in a line in front of the empty bowl on the left. Give each child a cup.

Say: **Let's have a snack that helps us see how the disciples may've felt when they caught all those fish. The disciples fished all night and weren't able to catch anything.** Give each child a turn at trying to scoop a snack out of the empty bowl on the left. **When the disciples followed Jesus' instructions to throw their net on the right-hand side of the boat, they caught a lot of fish.** Help kids scoop a snack out of the full bowl on the right. Let kids sit down, pray, and eat.

Ask:

- *What was it like when you didn't get a snack the first time?*
- *What was it like when you were able to scoop up fish from the other bowl?*

Say: **When the disciples first saw Jesus on the beach, they didn't know who he was. But they still listened to him and did what he told them to do. They were glad they listened and obeyed. We can obey Jesus, too.**

# Obey

**SUPPLIES**

## Song

**S**ay: **Let's sing a song about obeying Jesus.** Teach preschoolers the following words and motions to the tune of "Twinkle, Twinkle, Little Star."

Sing:

**I will, I will, I'll obey.** *(nod head up and down)*

**Jesus help me; this I pray.** *(fold hands in prayer)*

**Help me see you do great things.** *(point to eyes)*

**That is what obeying brings.** *(spread arms out wide)*

**I will, I will, I'll obey.** *(nod head up and down)*

**Jesus help me, this I pray.** *(fold hands in prayer)*

# So Many Fish!

## Action Play

**SUPPLIES**

**R**ead your preschoolers the following rhyme about the miraculous catch of fish, having them follow along as you do the actions in parentheses while you read each line.

Rhyme:

**Simon Peter and a few good friends** *(hold hands with someone)*

**Swam out one day to a boat to spend** *(make swimming motions with arms)*

**Some time there fishing with a net,** *(throw hands out in front)*

**But by morning, they hadn't caught one yet.** *(shake head no)*

**Jesus called out from the beach.** *(cup hands around mouth)*

**His voice was loud enough to reach.** *(cup hand behind ears)*

**Jesus asked, "Did you catch any fish?"** *(hold hands out to sides, palms up)*

**Simon Peter just said, "No, but I wish!"** *(shake head no)*

**"Switch your nets to the right-hand side,"** *(raise right hand above head)*

**Jesus told them. So they tried,** *(cup hands around mouth)*

**And caught so many fish in their net** *(make a circle with arms in front)*

**Simon Peter decided to get wet!** *(jump forward and hold nose as if jumping in water)*

**SUPPLIES**

## Prayer

**H**ave kids stand in a circle with you and hold hands.

Say: **Jesus encouraged the disciples when he appeared to them. He encouraged them by helping them find fish to catch. He encouraged them by spending time with them.**

Ask:

- *When have you been encouraged by someone?*
- *What are some ways you can encourage others?*

Say: **Let's pray together that Jesus will help us be encouraging to others.** Go around the circle and have kids name someone they can encourage. After everyone has shared, pray the following prayer.

Pray:

**Dear Jesus, thank you for the ways you encourage us. Thank you that we can encourage others. Help us be encouraging to the people we meet. In your name we pray, amen.**

# Jesus Tells the Parable of the Lost Son

## Luke 15:1-2, 11-32

### The Younger Son Wants His Way

#### Bible Experience

**SUPPLIES**

Bible, play money

**H**ave children sit in a circle with you. Open your Bible to Luke 15, and show children the words. Tell them the Bible is God's special book.

Say: **The Bible says Jesus liked to tell stories.**

Ask:

- *What's your favorite story?*
- *What do you like about your favorite story?*

Say: **The kind of stories Jesus told were called parables. A parable is a little story that has a bigger meaning.**

**One parable Jesus told was about a father and his two sons. The sons knew that when their father died all his money would become theirs. But the younger son didn't want to wait until his father died to get the money. So one day the younger son told his father he wanted his part of the money now.** Give each child some play money to hold.

**After his father gave him the money, the younger son packed up his things and moved away to a distant land.** Have children pretend to pack their bags and walk happily around the room several times. **Then the younger son started to do bad things and wasted all the money his father had given him.** Have children give their play money back to you and sit down.

**Since the younger son didn't have any more money, he had to get a job feeding pigs.** Have kids stand up and pretend to be pigs.

**There was also a famine in the land. A famine is when there's no rain and plants won't grow. Because plants wouldn't grow, there wasn't much food. The son got so hungry he wished he could eat the food he was giving the pigs.** Have the children rub their tummies in hunger.

**The younger son remembered what it was like when he lived at home with his father. He realized even his father's servants had more to eat than he did. So he decided to go home to his father and tell his father he was sorry.**

Ask:

- *What do you think about Jesus' story?*
- *What do you think about what the son did?*

Say: **The younger son thought his father would be mad at him and wouldn't let him live at home again, but he decided to ask if he could come back and work for his father as a servant. But the father wasn't mad at him! Before the younger son even got to his father's house, the father saw him coming, ran to meet him, and gave him a huge hug.** Have children give each other hugs.

Ask:

- *What do you think about what the father did?*

Say: **The younger son tried to tell his father he was sorry. But the father was so happy his younger son was home, he didn't pay attention. The father got new clothes for his son to wear and threw a party.**

Ask:

- *What do you think about what the father did for the son?*

Say: **When the father threw a party because the younger son came home, the older son wasn't happy. He didn't think it was fair that he had stayed at home and helped his father and had never been given a party by his father. But now his father was throwing a party for the younger son, who had moved away and wasted all his father's money.**

Ask:

- *What do you think about how the older brother felt?*
- *Tell whether you agree or disagree with the older brother.*
- *Tell about a time in your family that you felt someone or something was unfair.*

Say: **The older son was so mad that he wouldn't even go to the party. The father told the older son he should be happy his brother came home and was safe now.**

THE **GIANT** BOOK OF PRESCHOOL IDEAS FOR CHILDREN'S MINISTRY

We don't know if the older son changed his mind and decided to be happy because his brother returned; Jesus didn't say. Jesus told this story because he wanted us to think about how God feels when people decide they want God to be their friend. We can welcome those people with love just like the father in the story welcomed and accepted the younger son when he came home. In Jesus' story, the father is like God.

Ask:

- *What does this story help you learn about what God is like?*

Say: **God loves to see us follow and obey him, and he will always love us.**

# Who Am I?

## Craft

**SUPPLIES**
small paper plates, washable markers, craft sticks, tape

**G**ive a paper plate and a craft stick to each child, and set out markers to share. On the back of the plate, have children draw the face of someone from the parable of the lost son (father, younger son, older son, pig, servant, or whoever they choose). Try to make sure all the characters are covered.

Help children tape the craft stick to the back of the plate as a handle. If time allows, have children use their puppets to act out the parable.

# Son, Son, Come to the Party

## Game

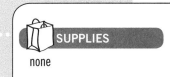

**SUPPLIES**
none

**S**ay: **Let's play a game like Duck, Duck, Goose to remember how the father wanted the older brother to be excited because the younger brother had come back home.**

Have children sit in a circle. Choose one child to stand outside the circle and be the "Father." Have the children in the circle close their eyes. The Father will walk around the circle tapping children lightly on their shoulders and saying "Son" each

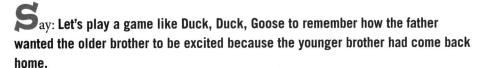

time he or she taps a shoulder. Whenever the Father chooses to, he or she will tap a shoulder and say, "Come to the party."

The child invited to the party will get up and chase the Father around the outside of the circle, trying to tag him or her. The Father will try to return to where the other child was sitting before being tagged. If the Father is tagged, he or she continues as the Father during the next round and the child invited to the party returns to his or her spot. If the Father is able to sit down before being tagged, the child invited to the party becomes the new Father. Repeat the game several times, making sure as many children as possible have an opportunity to participate.

When the game is over, ask children the following questions.

Ask:

- *When have you invited someone to a party?*
- *How did you choose who you would invite?*
- *What are some ways you can invite people to be friends with God?*

Say: **God wants to be friends with everyone!**

# Piggie Food

## Snack

**SUPPLIES**

clean bucket or pail, O-shaped cereal, pre-popped popcorn, napkins, antibacterial gel (optional)

ALLERGY ALERT!
See page 5

Say: **While the younger son lived away from his family, he didn't always have enough food to eat. It got so bad he even started thinking about eating the food he gave to the pigs. Let's have a snack that reminds us of the younger son's hunger.**

Make a snack mix of cereal and popcorn. Have children clean their hands, and place the mix in a clean bucket or pail to resemble a slop bucket used to feed pigs. Place a napkin in front of each child. Walk around and give each child a snack portion of the mix by taking a handful from the bucket and placing it on the napkins. Have children imagine they're the younger son in the parable and are so hungry they wish they could eat pigs' food. Say a prayer, thanking God for providing us food to eat.

Ask:

- *What kinds of foods do other animals eat?*
- *When you get really hungry, what kind of food do you like to eat?*

Say: **Because the younger son was hungry, he started thinking about going home to his father. He knew if he went back home he wouldn't be hungry anymore. And when he went home, his father celebrated that his younger son had come back.**

Ask:

- *Where do you go to get food when you're hungry?*
- *God gives us food when we're hungry. What else does God give us?*

Say: **God provides everything we need.**

# I Came Home

## Song

**SUPPLIES**

**Teacher TIP**

If you have more than 8 children, consider breaking into 2 or more groups to reduce the number of times you'd repeat the song.

**H**ave kids stand in a circle with you. Say: **Let's sing a song about what it's like to go home like the younger son in the parable did.**

Ask:

- *What would you miss if you left home?*

Go around the circle, letting each child answer.

Teach preschoolers the following words and motions to the tune of "Frère Jacques." As you sing and do the actions, lead kids walking in a circle as if they're traveling home. When you sing the lines "I miss my…" have kids stop walking and let one child have a turn filling in the blank. Repeat the song until each child has had an opportunity to fill in the blank. Change directions on occasion to keep things interesting.

Sing:

**I'm so hungry.** *(rub tummy)*

**I'm so cold.** *(wrap arms around body)*

**I'm so sad.** *(make sad faces and rub eyes with fists)*

**I'm so sad.** *(make sad faces and rub eyes with fists)*

**I miss my** [something a child would miss if he or she left home].
  *(stop walking as one child fills in the blank)*

**I miss my** [something a child would miss if he or she left home].
  *(have same child fill in the blank)*

**I'll go home.** *(march happily in a circle)*

**I'll go home.** *(march happily in a circle)*

# The Older Brother's Choice

## Action Play

**R**ead preschoolers the following rhyme about the older brother, having them follow along as you do the actions in parentheses while you read each line.

Rhyme:

**I hear music,** *(cup hand to ear)*

**Why all this fun?** *(hold hands out to sides, palms up)*

**I've worked all day** *(pretend to shovel)*

**Out in the sun.** *(wipe forehead with back of hand)*

**They say, "Let's dance!"** *(skip in place)*

**My brother's found.** *(cover hands with eyes; then uncover them)*

**I won't go in.** *(shake head no)*

**I'll stand my ground.** *(cross arms on chest)*

**My dad says, "Come."** *(wave to self)*

**He loves me, too.** *(point to self)*

**Should I go in?** *(walk in place)*

**What would you do?** *(point to someone)*

*(Encourage children to answer that question.)*

# Celebration Prayer

## Prayer

**H**ave children gather and sit in a circle with you. Give each child a party hat and a noisemaker.

Say: **Jesus told the parable of the lost son to remind people to be excited when others choose to follow God. Let's have a celebration for good reasons to follow God.**

Go around the circle, letting each child share a reason it's good to follow God. After each child shares, have the rest of the kids blow their noisemakers and cheer. After everyone has had an opportunity to share, tell kids you're excited each of them is present to learn about Jesus with you. Blow your noisemaker and cheer for them.

Close your time with the following prayer.

Pray:

**Thank you, God, that you celebrate when we choose to follow you. Help us celebrate when others choose to follow you, too. Thank you for every boy and girl here today. We love you. In Jesus' name, amen.**

# Jesus Befriends Zacchaeus

## Luke 19:1-10

## Jesus Sees Zacchaeus

### Bible Experience

**G**ather children in a circle on the floor with you. Open your Bible to Luke 19, and show children the words. Tell them the Bible is God's special book.

Say: **The Bible tells about a man named Zacchaeus. Zacchaeus was a rich man who was the chief tax collector, which meant he took money from everyone.**

**In those days, people had to pay a tax to Rome.** Give 10 pennies to the children. **The tax collector's job was to collect the taxes from the people.** Take three pennies back. **Zacchaeus would take part of the tax for himself.** Take another penny and put it in your pocket. **Sometimes he would take more from the people than he should have so he would get a little extra.** Take another penny and put it in your pocket. **That's how Zacchaeus got to be so rich. It's also why people didn't like him very much.**

**One day Zacchaeus heard that Jesus was coming through his town. He wanted to see Jesus. But there was a crowd, and Zacchaeus was a short man.**

Ask:

- *When have you wanted to see something but something or someone blocked your view?*
- *How were you able to see what you wanted to see?*

Say: **Zacchaeus knew where Jesus was going. So Zacchaeus ran ahead of the crowd and climbed a sycamore-fig tree.** Have children pretend to climb a tree and then sit on the branches and limbs. Have them look around to see Jesus.

**When Jesus reached the tree Zacchaeus had climbed, he stopped. Jesus looked up at Zacchaeus and told Zacchaeus to come down. Jesus wanted to be a guest in Zacchaeus' home. So Zacchaeus quickly climbed down the tree and took Jesus to his house. Zacchaeus was very happy Jesus was going to be his guest.** Have children pretend to climb down the tree. Then lead children in skipping and jumping for joy around the room a few times. Lead children to the blanket-covered table and have them sit down in front of it. Tell kids the table is Zacchaeus' house.

**When the crowd of people saw Jesus go home with Zacchaeus, they were angry.** Have kids make angry faces. **They didn't think Jesus should be spending time with a man like Zacchaeus—a man who stole from them. What the people couldn't see is Zacchaeus had changed in his heart. He really wanted to make God happy.**

**On the way to his house, Zacchaeus stopped and told Jesus he would give half of all his possessions to the poor.** Put the 10 pennies in a line on the table where kids can see. Pick up half the pennies and tell children that's how much Zacchaeus was going to give the poor. Leave the remaining five pennies on the table. **Zacchaeus also told Jesus he would give back to the people he took too much money from. Zacchaeus wasn't going to just give back what he took. He was going to give back four times as much!**

**Jesus knew Zacchaeus was doing these things because he loved God. Zacchaeus didn't want to do bad things anymore. He wanted to follow Jesus and do things that made God happy.**

Ask:

- *What are some ways you can show God that you love him?*

Say: **Jesus told Zacchaeus the changes in Zacchaeus' heart showed that God had saved him. And that was the whole reason Jesus came—"to seek and save those who are lost."**

Ask:

- *What does this story help you learn about what God is like?*

# God Sees Me, Even in a Tree

## Craft

**SUPPLIES**

green construction paper triangles, brown chenille wires cut in half, foam cups, paper clips, small strips of skin-colored construction paper, washable markers, hole punch, scissors

**S**ay: **Let's make a tree to remember that God sees us all the time, just as he saw Zacchaeus when he was in a tree.**

Give six chenille wire halves and a foam cup to each child. Help children gently poke the chenille wires one by one through the bottom of the cup and spread out the wires to form tree branches.

Give children each several construction-paper triangles. These will be leaves for the tree. Help children punch a hole in one corner of each triangle, and then have children thread the leaves onto the branches.

Give children each a small strip of skin-colored construction paper, and help kids draw a simple face. Kids will use a paper clip to attach their face onto one of the tree branches.

**God loves us and sees us all the time, even if we don't think he can. He sees us when it's light or when it's dark. He sees us when we're happy or when we're sad. He sees us even if we're in a tree, like Zacchaeus was. He knows exactly what's happening in our lives, and God will always take care of us.** Have kids clap their hands to thank God for reminding us that he always sees us.

If time allows, have children use their craft to act out Zacchaeus' encounter with Jesus.

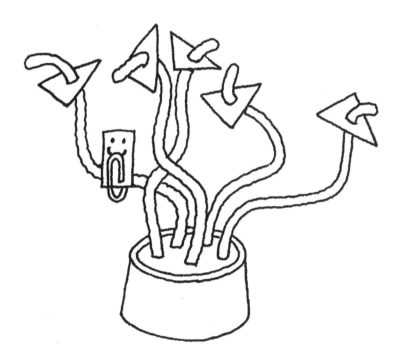

# What Do I See?

## Game

**SUPPLIES**

artificial tree, small step stool

**H**ave children sit facing an artificial tree. Place a step stool next to the tree and just behind it. Have children take turns being Zacchaeus looking for Jesus, pretending to climb the tree by standing on the stool and looking through the branches of the tree.

Have the child on the stool find an object in the room for the other kids to guess. Have him or her say, "I see something [color of the object]." If someone guesses correctly, have that child take Zacchaeus' place in the tree. If no one guesses correctly after three tries, have Zacchaeus tell the group what he or she saw. Then choose a new person to be Zacchaeus. Continue the game until everyone has had a turn in the tree.

When the game is over, discuss the following questions.

Ask:

- *What was it like to look out from a tree?*
- *What are some things you can do to look for Jesus?*
- *What are some ways you can help others see Jesus?*

Say: **It's good for us to always look for Jesus!**

# We Can Share

## Snack

**SUPPLIES**

large bowl, raisins, O-shaped cereal, Chex cereal, resealable plastic bags, small paper plates, antibacterial gel (optional)

ALLERGY ALERT!
See page 5

**B**efore children arrive, create a snack mix of raisins, O-shaped cereal, and Chex cereal in a large bowl.

Say: **Zacchaeus was happy that Jesus wanted to be his friend and go to his house. When Zacchaeus heard the crowd complaining that Jesus shouldn't go to Zacchaeus' house because Zacchaeus was a bad man, Zacchaeus wanted to show**

**Jesus how much he loved God. He told Jesus he would give away half of everything he had. Let's make a snack to remind us that we can show God we love him by sharing what we have with others.**

Have children clean their hands before they prepare the snacks. Give each child a double serving of the snack mix on a paper plate. Also give each child an empty resealable plastic bag. Have children each put half their snack mix into the plastic bag, and then help seal it. Then let kids eat what's left on their plates and take the bag of snack mix with them to share with someone else later.

As kids prepare and eat their snacks, ask them who they're going to share their snack with later.

Ask:

- *Tell about a time someone shared something with you.*
- *What's it like when others share with you?*
- *What are some other things you can share?*

Say: **When we share with others, we're making God happy!**

# Zaccheaus Climbed a Tree

## Song

**SUPPLIES**

**S**ay: **Let's sing a song about Zacchaeus climbing a tree to see Jesus!** Teach preschoolers the following words and motions to the tune of "The Bear Went Over the Mountain."

Sing:

**Zacchaeus climbed a tree,** *(climb with arms and legs)*

**Zacchaeus climbed a tree,** *(climb with arms and legs)*

**Zacchaeus climbed a tree** *(climb with arms and legs)*

**To see what he could see.** *(shade eyes with hands)*

**What did he hope to see?** *(hold arms to sides, palms up)*

**What did he hope to see?** *(hold arms to sides, palms up)*

**Zacchaeus was looking for Jesus.** (*shade eyes with hands and look around*)

**Zacchaeus was looking for Jesus.** (*shade eyes with hands and look around*)

**Zacchaeus was looking for Jesus.** (*shade eyes with hands and look around*)

**That's why he climbed the tree.** (*climb with arms and legs*)

**Jesus saw Zacchaeus,** (*shade eyes with hands and look up*)

**Jesus saw Zacchaeus,** (*shade eyes with hands and look up*)

**Jesus saw Zacchaeus** (*shade eyes with hands and look up*)

**And said, "Come down to me."** (*wave to self*)

**Zacchaeus came down the tree.** (*climb with arms and legs*)

**Zacchaeus came down the tree.** (*climb with arms and legs*)

**"I'll go to your house today.** (*walk in place*)

**"I'll go to your house today.** (*walk in place*)

**"I'll go to your house today."** (*walk in place*)

**Zacchaeus said, "Wee-hee!"** (*jump up and down*)

# A New Friend for Jesus

**SUPPLIES**

## Action Play

**R**ead preschoolers the following rhyme about Zacchaeus, having them follow along as you do the actions in parentheses while you read each line.

Rhyme:

**Zacchaeus was short—not very tall—**(*hold hand waist high, palm down*)

**So he couldn't see Jesus at all.** (*cover eyes with hands*)

**Jesus was preaching to a crowd** (*cup hands around mouth*)

**When Zacchaeus thought out loud:** (*point to forehead*)

**"Although I cannot see from here,** *(shake head no)*

**On that branch, I would be near.** *(point up)*

**From in that tree, there I could see."** *(shade eyes with hands)*

**So Zacchaeus climbed up a sycamore tree.** *(climb with arms and legs)*

**And he was right; there he could see.** *(nod head yes)*

**And Jesus saw him in that tree.** *(shade eyes with hands, looking up)*

**"Come down, Zacchaeus," Jesus said.** *(wave to self)*

**"Let's go to your home. Let's break some bread."** *(walk in place)*

**Zacchaeus climbed down that tree real fast.** *(climb down with arms and legs)*

**He ran to Jesus; the crowd walked past.** *(run in place)*

**Zacchaeus and Jesus walked side by side.** *(walk in place next to someone)*

**Zacchaeus stood tall and beamed with pride.** *(stand up tall)*

# God Sees Me

## Prayer

**SUPPLIES**

hand mirror

**H**ave children sit in a circle with you.

Say: **The people didn't like Zacchaeus. When they looked at him, they saw a tax collector—someone they thought was their enemy. When Jesus saw Zacchaeus, he saw someone he loved—someone he wanted as a friend. He sees us the same way.**

Pass a hand mirror around the circle. Have children take turns looking at themselves in the mirror. As children look into the mirror, have them pray—thanking God that he loves them and wants to be their friend.

After everyone has had a turn, close the time with a prayer of your own, also thanking God for every child in the group and that you get to spend time with them each week.

# Jesus Enters Jerusalem as King

## Mark 11:1-11

### Jesus Is Honored

## Bible Experience

**SUPPLIES**

Bible, 1 bath towel per child

**G**ather children together, and provide each child with a bath towel to sit on. Open your Bible to Mark 11, and show children the words. Tell them the Bible is God's special book.

Say: **Today we'll discover what the Bible says happened on a day Jesus came into Jerusalem. Jesus and his disciples had traveled a long way.**

Ask:

- *When have you gone on a long trip?*
- *What's it like to travel a long way?*

Say: **As they got close to the city, Jesus sent two of the disciples ahead to find a donkey.** Have children make donkey sounds. **Jesus told them exactly where to find the donkey.**

**When the disciples brought the donkey to Jesus, they laid their coats on the donkey's back for Jesus to sit on. Then Jesus rode the donkey the rest of the way into Jerusalem.**

Ask:

- *What ways do people travel today?*
- *What is your favorite way to travel?*

Say: **A long time before Jesus lived on earth, the Bible said the special one who'd save God's people would ride into Jerusalem on a donkey. That's exactly what Jesus did.**

Ask:

- *Who are some people you think are special and important today?*

Say: **For someone as important as Jesus, riding a donkey was kind of strange. Most important people would've found a fancier way to travel. As Jesus rode along, people started to put their coats and other things such as palm branches on the road for the donkey to walk on.** Have children stand and make two rows facing each other. Have them place their towels on the floor in the space between the two rows, creating a long walkway between. Have children sit back down in their rows next to the towels. **In those days, laying coats and other things in the road to walk on was something people did for kings and other important people. When they did this for Jesus, they were showing they believed he was very special and important.**

Ask:

- *What are ways we show people they're important to us?*

Say: **Many people gathered to watch Jesus as he rode by. They shouted praises to God, because they knew he was special. We know he's special, too. Let's shout our own praises to Jesus now.** Lead kids in a parade around the room. Walk down the towel walkway two or three times during the parade. As you march, lead kids in shouting out things like "Hosannah!" or "Jesus, you are king!"

# I Praise God

## Craft

**SUPPLIES**

1 copy per child of the "I Praise God" handout (at the end of this chapter), green construction paper, glue sticks, pen or pencil, music player and upbeat preschool-friendly praise music

**S**ay: **When Jesus entered Jerusalem, the people who saw him shouted praises to God. Let's make a craft to help us remember we can still praise Jesus today.**

Give each child a copy of the "I Praise God" handout and a piece of green construction paper. Set out glue sticks. Help children write their names on their handouts, and then have children create a palm branch by tearing pieces of construction paper and gluing them to the picture of the palm branch on their handout. Play praise music in the background while children work.

As children are finishing up their palm branches, talk about the following questions.

Ask:

- *What's something you praise God for?* Help kids write their responses on the space at the bottom of the handout.
- *Why is it important that we praise God?*
- *What are ways we can praise God?*

Say: **We can still praise God—just like the people did when Jesus entered Jerusalem as king.**

# Riding a Donkey

## Game

**SUPPLIES**

table runner; stuffed animals; towels, coats, or palm branches made in the "I Praise God" activity

**T**he goal of the game is for a child, on hands and knees acting like a donkey, to carry a stuffed animal down an aisle on his or her back without the animal falling off. If the stuffed animal falls off, the other children can help put it back on. The other children will play the cheering crowd to encourage the donkey.

Have the children stand on each side of the table runner that you've laid out on the floor. Each child will have either a towel, coat, or palm branch to wave and lay out for the donkey to walk on. One child will play the part of the donkey. Let the child attempt to carry the stuffed animal down the aisle on his or her back with help as needed. Repeat this until each child has a turn. If you have a large group, consider having more than one child at a time play the part of a donkey, one behind the other.

Say: **Let's imagine we're watching someone ride on a donkey like Jesus did.** (Send the "donkey" down the aisle.)

**Say nice things and helpful words to encourage the donkey. If the stuffed animal falls off, you can help put it back on the donkey.**

Give every child a turn to be the donkey.

Ask:

- *How hard was it for you to keep the stuffed animal on your back?*

Say: **The donkey Jesus rode had never before been ridden, so it might've been difficult for Jesus because the donkey wasn't used to having someone on its back.**

Ask:

- *Describe how you felt to hear your friends cheer for you.*
- *What would you say to encourage Jesus if he were here now?*

Say: **Jesus was a real person who rode a real donkey. People cheered for him that day, too!**

# Fruit Snack Fun

## Snack

**SUPPLIES**

paper plates, 1 Fruit Roll-Up and 2 animal crackers per child, music player and upbeat preschool-friendly praise music, antibacterial gel (optional)

ALLERGY ALERT!
See page 5

**H**ave children clean their hands before they prepare the snacks, and then ask children to pray with you, praising God for the snack.

Say: **Tear your fruit roll-up into pieces and put the pieces on your plate. Now make a path in the middle of your plate just as the people did when Jesus came to town, and pick up one of your animal crackers.**

**Let's make this animal cracker walk down the path while we praise Jesus.** Have kids say with you, **"Let's praise Jesus, who comes in the name of God!"**

While children enjoy eating the snack, play praise songs. Talk with the children about what they are thankful for as they eat.

# Hallelu, Hallelu

## Song

SUPPLIES

palm branches made in the "I Praise God" activity

**S**ay: **Today we've been praising Jesus and learning that the people were very happy when Jesus came into Jerusalem. They said, "Praise God! Blessings on the one who comes in the name of the Lord!"**

Have preschoolers form two lines facing each other. Teach kids on one side to sing "Hallelu, Hallelu!" as they wave their palm branches.

Teach the kids on the other side to sing "Praise ye the Lord!" as they wave their palm branches back.

Let the kids have fun chanting back and forth while they wave their palm branches.

# Jesus Rides a Colt

## Action Play

SUPPLIES

**R**ead preschoolers the following rhyme about Jesus' triumphant entry, encouraging them to follow along as you do the actions in parentheses while you read each line.

Rhyme:

**Jesus and his friends were walking.** *(walk in place)*

**Jesus and his friends were talking.** *(hold hand in front of you; then open and close fingers)*

**"You two go ahead,"** *(thrust pointer finger forward)*

**Jesus said.** *(cup hands around mouth)*

**"You will see a colt nearby** *(shade eyes with hands and look around)*

**That you will have to untie.** *(hold fists in front and circle them around each other)*

**Bring it here.** *(motion to self)*

**Have no fear.** *(sweep pointer finger back and forth in front)*

**Say, 'I'll return it very soon—**(*hold hands together in front, palms up*)

**Yet this very afternoon.' "** (*tap wrist with finger*)

**Jesus rode to town.** (*hold fists together in front as if holding reins, and bounce at the knees*)

**People saw him and bowed down.** (*bow*)

**They laid palm branches in his way.** (*squat down, and pretend to lay something on the floor*)

**The donkey he just walked and brayed.** (*put hands on head, pointer fingers up, to make donkey ears*)

**Heard far and wide,** (*cup hands to ears*)

**"Hosannah!" people cried.** (*put hands above head, palms open*)

# Body Prayer

## Prayer

**SUPPLIES**

**G**ather kids together.

Say: **When Jesus rode the donkey into Jerusalem, people praised God with their voices. Let's use other parts of our bodies to praise him, too.**

Have kids repeat the following prayer and motions after you. Tell kids that after they repeat each part of the prayer, you'll allow time for them to praise God with the part of their bodies mentioned in the prayer.

Pray:

**Lord, I want to praise you with my lips.** Point to your lips. **Lord, I want to praise you with my heart.** Put your hands on your heart. **Lord, I want my hands to praise you.** Hold your hands out in front, palms up. **Lord, I want to praise you with my whole life.** Raise your hands above your head. **We praise you, God, because you're our king. Thank you for loving us. Thank you for saving us. In Jesus' name, amen.**

# I Praise God

"Praise God! Blessings on the one who comes in the name of the Lord!"
Mark 11:9

I praise God for _____.

# Jesus' Last Supper With His Friends

## Mark 14:12-26

## A Special Meal

### Bible Experience

 **SUPPLIES**

Bible, bread, red grape juice, clear plastic cup

**G**ather kids together. Open your Bible to Mark 14, and show children the words. Tell them the Bible is God's special book.

Say: **The Bible tells about a special dinner Jesus had with his disciples. It was the beginning of the Passover—a special holiday when Jewish people celebrate God saving his people. Jesus sent two of his friends to find a place where they could eat their Passover meal.** Have kids pretend they are getting ready to have people over for a big meal. They can do things like pick up toys, pretend to set a table, make food, or whatever they'd like. As they play, talk about the following questions.

Ask:

- *Where does your family eat special meals?*
- *Who gets things ready for your family celebrations?*

Gather kids again, and have them sit in a circle with you.

Say: **The two friends found a place for the Passover meal. And that evening Jesus and all 12 friends gathered together to eat. While they were eating, Jesus began to tell his friends that one of them would leave him and wouldn't be his friend anymore.**

Ask:

- *What do you think about knowing one of Jesus' friends would leave him?*

Say: **The friends were shocked! None of them believed they could stop being Jesus' friend. Jesus didn't say who it would be—only that it was someone who was having supper with him that night.**

**A little later Jesus did something very special. He took a piece of bread from the table, tore it up, and gave it to his disciples.** Hold up piece of bread and show it to the kids. **When Jesus did this, he told the disciples the bread was his body, because his body would be broken apart just like he broke the bread.**

**Then Jesus picked up a drink, gave thanks for it, and gave it to his friends as well.** Hold up the clear cup of grape juice to show the kids. **Jesus said the drink was like his blood, because his blood would be poured out just like a drink pours out of a cup. And when his body was broken and his blood poured out, people could be friends with God again.**

Ask:

- *Why do you think Jesus cared about his friends so much?*

Say: **When Jesus gave bread and drink to his disciples, he started something we still do today called communion. When we eat bread and drink juice, we are doing the same thing Jesus did with his disciples at that Passover meal.**

**When their supper was over, Jesus and the disciples sang a song about God.**

Ask:

- *What is your favorite song to sing about Jesus?*
- *What do you like best about it?*

Sing some of the songs kids mention. If you're unfamiliar with the songs, invite willing children to sing the songs for you if they know them.

# Remembrance Placemats

## Craft

**SUPPLIES**

1 copy per child of the "Last Supper" handout (at the end of this chapter), 11 x 17 sheets of construction paper, crayons, glue sticks, contact paper, scissors

**Teacher TIP**

Make one copy of the "Last Supper" handout, and then cut it out where indicated. Enlarge the trimmed copy to 150 percent, and make enough copies for each child to have one.

**S**ay: **When Jesus and the disciples ate the Last Supper, Jesus told the disciples he wanted them to remember that he died for them. Let's make placemats to help us remember Jesus loves us and died for us, too.**

Give each child a copy of the "Last Supper" handout. Help children write their names on their handouts, and let children color the picture in any way they choose. When children are finished coloring, help them glue the colored picture to a piece of construction paper. Place clear contact paper over the front and back of their pictures to preserve them.

Ask:

- *When do you have special meals with your family?*
- *What kinds of foods do you eat at those meals?*
- *Jesus gave his friends special food so they would remember he died for them. What are other ways you can remember Jesus died for you?*

Say: **Jesus loves each one of us and died for us. Let's always remember that.**

# Memory Play

## Game

**SUPPLIES**

copies of the "Memory Play" handout (at the end of this chapter), scissors

**B**efore children arrive, cut apart the pictures in the "Memory Play" handout. Cut enough pictures for each child to have one. It's okay if two or more children have the same picture.

Say: **Let's play a memory game.**

Give each child one picture from the "Memory Play" handout. Explain to kids that each picture reminds us of something about Jesus. As you explain each picture, have the kids who received that picture hold it up for everyone to see.

Say:

- **The heart reminds us Jesus loves us very much.**
- **The cross reminds us Jesus gave his life for us.**
- **The smiley face reminds us Jesus forgives us.**
- **The cloud reminds us Jesus is the way to heaven.**

Have children each look at their picture for 30 seconds and remember what it is. Collect all the pictures, mix them up, and give each child a new picture. Instruct kids to mingle with one another to find their original pictures and retrieve them. Have children sit down when they have their original pictures back and have returned the second picture they were given to its original owner.

Ask:

- *What was this game like for you?*
- *How did you remember which picture you had?*
- *How do bread and juice remind us that Jesus died for us?*

Say: **Jesus told his disciples to remember he loved them and died for them. He gave them bread and juice to help them remember. Remember he loves you and died for you, too.**

# Dinner With Jesus

## Snack

**SUPPLIES**

crackers, sliced seedless grapes, cheese spread, foam or paper bowls, plastic spoons, music player and upbeat preschool-friendly praise music, antibacterial gel (optional)

*ALLERGY ALERT!*
See page 5

Have children clean their hands before they eat their snacks. Give each child several sliced grapes in a bowl along with several crackers and cheese spread. Tell children the crackers are like the bread Jesus gave his disciples at the Last Supper. Tell children the grapes are like the wine Jesus gave his disciples, because wine—like grape juice—is made from smashed grapes.

Let kids dip their crackers in the cheese spread just as Jesus and the disciples dipped their bread as they ate. Play praise music in the background as children enjoy their snack.

While children eat, talk about the following questions.

Ask:

- *What other food do you think Jesus and the disciples ate besides bread and wine?*
- *What kinds of things does your family do when you eat together?*
- *Why do you think it's important for us to remember Jesus died for us?*

Say: **Let's always remember what Jesus did for us—and how much he loves us.**

# Jesus Loves Me, He Invites Me Close

## Song

**SUPPLIES**

heart stickers, song "Jesus Loves Me" and music player (optional)

**S**ay: **Let's sing "Jesus Loves Me"—but with a twist!**

Sing:

**Jesus loves me!**

**This I know, for the Bible tells me so;**

**Little ones to him belong;**

**They are weak, but he is strong.**

**Yes, Jesus loves me!**

**Yes, Jesus loves me!**

**Yes, Jesus loves me!**

**The Bible tells me so.**

Say: **Now let's learn another verse to this song.**

Sing:

**Jesus loves me!**

**He invites me close;**

**To be with him is what I chose.**

**He will teach me every day;**

**And I will remember him today!**

**Yes, Jesus loves me!**

**Yes, Jesus loves me!**

**Yes, Jesus loves me!**

**The Bible tells me so.**

While they sing this song, place a heart sticker on each child's shoulder.

# Jesus Love You Very Much

## Action Play

**C**ut apart the "Memory Play" handout, or use one set of the pictures you cut out for the "Memory Play" game. Each of the pictures in the "Memory Play" handout is used in the rhyme. Show the pictures as you read each line.

Rhyme:

**Jesus loves you very much** *(hold up picture of a heart)*

**And wants you to remember** *(point to your temple on each word)*

**He gave his life** *(hold up picture of a cross)*

**So we can be forgiven** *(hold up picture of the smiley face)*

**and go to heaven.** *(hold up picture of the cloud)*

Repeat the lines with the kids.

Say: **You did a great job remembering these important words!**

## Picture Prayer

### Prayer

**H**ave kids sit in a circle with you to pray. Set the four pictures from the "Memory Play" handout on the floor in the center of the circle and explain what each picture reminds us of: The heart reminds us that Jesus loves us very much; the cross reminds us that Jesus gave his life for us; the smiley face reminds us that Jesus forgives us; and the cloud reminds us that Jesus is the way to heaven.

Go around the circle, asking kids to pray. Have children take turns saying which picture they like best and why and then praying a prayer of thanks for what that picture reminds them of.

Close the time with a prayer of thanks for the kids in your group and the time you have with them.

# Last Supper

### "I will remember Jesus' love."

**Mark 14:12-26**

Permission to photocopy this page from *The Giant Book of Preschool Ideas for Children's Ministry* granted for local church use.
Copyright © Group Publishing, Inc. group.com

# Memory Play

THE **GIANT** BOOK OF PRESCHOOL IDEAS FOR CHILDREN'S MINISTRY

# Jesus Dies on the Cross

## Mark 15:25-38

## Jesus on the Cross

### Bible Experience

**SUPPLIES**

Bible, small bowl of vinegar, piece of paper, antibacterial gel (optional)

ALLERGY ALERT!
See page 5

Open your Bible to Mark 15. Show children the words and tell them the Bible is God's special book. Explain that they'll experience the Bible as you tell what happened.

Say: **It was about 9 o'clock in the morning when soldiers put Jesus on the cross. The soldiers put a sign over Jesus' head that said "King of the Jews." And the soldiers put Jesus' cross between the crosses of two criminals.** Have kids spread out on the floor and lie down with their arms out to their sides in the shape of the cross. Then have kids look to the left and then the right, as Jesus hung on the cross between two criminals.

**As Jesus hung on the cross, many people walked by and made fun of him. They made fun of things Jesus had said—saying he wasn't really able to do the things he said he could. Even the criminals hanging next to Jesus said mean things to him.**

Ask:

- *Share about a time someone made fun of you or laughed at you.*
- *How was your experience like the people making fun of Jesus while he hung on the cross?*

Say: **At noon—when it was about lunchtime for everyone else—it turned very dark outside.** Turn off the lights.

**It stayed dark for three hours. By the end of that time, Jesus was very tired and felt like God wasn't with him anymore. So he yelled out. He asked, "Father, Father, why have you left me?"**

**When Jesus yelled out, people thought he was talking to one of the prophets from the Old Testament named Elijah. Then one of the people took a sponge, soaked it in some sour wine, and gave it to Jesus to drink.**

Ask:

- *Think about what it would be like to drink something really sour when you're very thirsty.*

Have kids clean their hands, and then walk around with a bowl of vinegar and encourage kids to each dip a finger in and taste it.

Say: **After this, Jesus took his last breath and died. The moment he died, something amazing happened. A huge curtain that hung in the Temple tore from top to bottom, because Jesus' death made it possible for anyone to come to God.**

Ask:

- *What does it mean to you that Jesus was willing to go through all this for you?*
- *What would you like to say to Jesus for what he did for you?*

Say: **Jesus loves you so much that he was willing to die on the cross for you. No matter what you do, Jesus will always love you.**

# Heart Cross

## Craft

**SUPPLIES**

red construction paper hearts, 2 craft sticks per child, glue sticks

**S**ay: **Let's make something to remind us of what Jesus did for us on the cross.**

Give each child two craft sticks. Show kids how to form a cross using the two craft sticks. Help kids glue the craft sticks together. Then give kids each several construction-paper hearts. Let kids glue the hearts to their crosses.

For each heart, ask kids to think of something they've done wrong. As they glue the hearts to their crosses, remind kids that Jesus loves them even when they do wrong things. Tell them Jesus loves them so much he died on the cross so they can be forgiven for the wrong things they do.

Ask:

- *What's it like to know all the wrong things you've done can be forgiven?*
- *What does it mean to you to know that Jesus loves you so much?*

Say: **No matter what, Jesus always loves you!**

# Forgiveness Tag

## Game

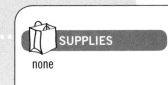

**SUPPLIES**

**S**ay: **Let's play a version of Freeze Tag called Forgiveness Tag.**

Choose one child to be the Tagger. Explain to kids that as they're tagged, they'll freeze—standing up—with their arms spread out in the shape of a cross.

**Here's the catch: At any time, I can choose to take a frozen child's place by tagging him or her—saying "You're forgiven"—and standing in the shape of the cross. Once I do this, that person can join the game again.**

Replace children during this game. After about 10 seconds, unfreeze yourself, choose another frozen child, and take his or her place. After a few minutes of play, choose another child to be the Tagger and continue playing.

When the game is over, have kids sit down wherever they are.

Ask:

- *What was it like to be frozen?*
- *How is what I did when I took a frozen child's place like what Jesus did for us on the cross?*

Say: **We've all done things that are wrong. Because of those wrong things, we deserve to be punished and die for our sin. However, Jesus took our place by dying on the cross for us.** Have kids clap their hands to thank God for taking our place by dying on the cross.

# Wrapped in Love

## Snack

**SUPPLIES**

thin pretzel sticks, red pull 'n' peel licorice, small paper plates, antibacterial gel (optional)

ALLERGY ALERT!
See page 5

**H**ave children clean their hands, and give them each two pretzel sticks and a piece of red pull 'n' peel licorice on a plate. Show kids how to use two thin pretzel sticks to form the shape of a cross. Then help kids wrap the sticks together with the piece of licorice. Tell kids that when Jesus bled and died on the cross, he wrapped us in his love and forgiveness.

Ask:

- *How does Jesus show his love for us?*
- *Tell about a time you've felt loved by Jesus.*

Let kids eat and enjoy their pretzel snack.

Say: **Jesus showed his love for you and me when he died on the cross. Jesus always loves us.**

# On the Cross

## Song

**SUPPLIES**

**S**ay: **Let's sing a song about Jesus and how he died on the cross for us.** Teach preschoolers the following words to the tune of "Frère Jacques."

Sing:

**Are you Jesus, are you Jesus,**

**On the cross? On the cross?** *(hold arms out like a cross)*

**For my sin, for your sin,**

**Jesus died for our sins,**

**On the cross. On the cross.** *(hold arms out like a cross)*

# Last Breath

## Action Play

**SUPPLIES**

**R**ead preschoolers the following rhyme about Jesus dying on the cross, having them follow along as you do the actions in parentheses while you read each line.

Rhyme:

**They hung Jesus on the cross at nine.** *(hold up nine fingers)*

**And above his head they placed a sign.** *(hold hands above head)*

**People walking by made fun of him.** *(walk in place)*

**And at noon the sky went dim.** *(place hand over eyes)*

**Then Jesus breathed his last breath,** *(take a deep breath)*

**And the Temple curtain tore at his death.** *(lie on the ground)*

# Hug Prayer

## Prayer

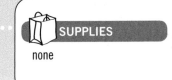

**SUPPLIES**

**T**alk with kids.

Ask:

- *What's it like when you know you've done something wrong?*
- *What's it like when your parents say "I forgive you" and give you a big hug?*

Say: **Let's thank God for sending Jesus to die for us on a cross and forgive all the bad things we do.**

Encourage kids to wrap their arms around themselves in a hug as they pray. After leading the children in prayer, have a big group hug.

# Jesus Rises on the Third Day

## Mark 16:1-8

## Empty Tomb

### Bible Experience

**SUPPLIES**

Bible, 4 white plastic cups, spice jar containing cinnamon or allspice, stone, angel shape or picture

**B**efore kids arrive, turn four white plastic cups upside down. Hide a spice jar under the first cup. Hide a stone under the second cup. Hide an angel shape or picture under the third one. The fourth cup will be empty.

Gather kids around the cups. Open your Bible to Mark 16, and show children the words. Explain to kids that after Jesus died on the cross, his body was put in a tomb—a cave used in those days for burying people.

Say: **These cups are like the tomb Jesus was buried in. One at a time, we'll open each tomb and discover something under each one that has to do with what happened in the Bible.**

Have a child open the first "tomb." Have kids take turns looking at and smelling the spice while you tell what happened.

**On the first day of the week, three women who knew Jesus—Mary Magdalene, Mary the mother of James, and Salome—took spices to Jesus' tomb to put on his body.**

Have another child open the next tomb. Encourage kids to pass the stone around as you tell what happened.

As the women walked to the tomb, they wondered how they were going to move the stone that covered the tomb. The stone was very heavy. But when they got to the tomb, they were surprised to discover the stone had already been moved.

Have another child open the third tomb. Let children pass around the angel while you tell what happened.

**The three women entered the tomb and were amazed to find a young man sitting in the tomb wearing all white—an angel!**

Have another child open the fourth tomb. Allow time for kids to express surprise over the empty tomb. Then continue telling what happened while kids pass around the empty tomb.

**The angel told the women that Jesus had risen and showed them the place where Jesus had lain. But Jesus wasn't there. The tomb was empty. What surprising and amazing news! Jesus is alive!** Have kids jump up and down and cheer in celebration.

Ask:

- *What do you think about what we just heard?*
- *What surprised you the most?*
- *What did you learn about how amazing Jesus is?*

Say: **Jesus is alive—and he wants to be your friend!**

# Angel Megaphone

## Craft

**SUPPLIES**

yellow or white construction paper, coffee filters, tape, washable markers

**S**ay: **Let's make something to help us remember the good news the angel told Mary at the tomb.**

Help kids each roll a piece of yellow or white construction paper to form a megaphone. Once the paper is rolled, tape it so it stays in place. Then have kids each take one coffee filter and pinch the center of it to make wings. Help kids tape the coffee-filter wings to the middle of the megaphone to create an angel.

Using markers, help kids draw faces on their angels. Then encourage kids to use their megaphones to share the good news the angel shared with Mary: Jesus is alive!

# Sad to Surprised

## Game

**SUPPLIES**

small opaque plastic container with lid, 1 sticker per child, music player and upbeat preschool-friendly praise music

**B**efore kids arrive, place an assortment of individual stickers inside an opaque plastic container and put on the lid.

Say: **When Mary went to the tomb that morning, she was sad because Jesus had died. She wasn't expecting the surprise waiting for her inside the tomb. Let's play a version of Hot Potato as you imagine what that may have been like for Mary.**

Have kids sit in a circle. Encourage kids to put on their best sad faces. Hand one child the container. Start the music, and encourage kids to pass the container as quickly as possible so they aren't still holding it when the music stops. After a couple of seconds, stop the music and have the child holding the container open it and find the surprise. Encourage children to express their surprise and excitement as that child removes a sticker. Close the container, have kids put on their sad faces, and start the music again. Play until every child has a turn to discover a surprise inside.

Ask:

- *What was it like for you playing this game?*
- *How is your experience from this game like what Mary experienced at the tomb?*

Say: **The tomb was supposed to be a sad place, but it turned into a joyful place because Jesus is alive!**

# Resurrection Rolls

## Snack

**SUPPLIES**

refrigerated crescent roll dough, large marshmallows, butter (melted and cooled), equal parts cinnamon and sugar, 2 bowls, baking sheet, parchment paper or aluminum foil, access to an oven, antibacterial gel (optional)

**B**efore kids arrive, preheat an oven to 350 degrees. Lay parchment paper or aluminum foil on a baking sheet. Combine the cinnamon and sugar in a bowl, and place the melted and cooled butter in another bowl.

Have kids clean their hands before they prepare the snacks. Give each child an individual triangle of the unbaked crescent roll dough and a large marshmallow. Help children each wrap their dough around a marshmallow, pinch the edges of the dough tightly together, and roll the dough into a ball to ensure the melted marshmallow doesn't leak out. Show kids how to dip their rolls into the melted butter and then roll them in the cinnamon sugar. Place the rolls on the baking sheet.

Bake the rolls until golden brown, about 15-18 minutes. (You can do another activity while the rolls bake.) Allow them to cool.

Distribute the rolls, and have children each take a bite of their roll and see that the marshmallow has disappeared. Ask the following questions as kids eat their snacks.

Ask:

- *How are these rolls like or unlike Jesus' tomb?*
- *Why does it matter that Jesus' tomb was empty?*
- *What can you tell others about what you learned from the Bible today?*

Say: **Like our resurrection rolls, Jesus' tomb was empty! The great news is that Jesus is alive!**

# Mary and the Tomb

**SUPPLIES**

## Song

**S**ay: **Let's sing a song about Mary going to Jesus' tomb.** Teach preschoolers the following words and motions to the tune of "London Bridge."

Sing:

**Mary hurried to the tomb,** (*pump arms and mimic running*)

**To the tomb, to the tomb.** (*make an "O" with your hands*)

**Mary hurried to the tomb** (*pump arms and mimic running*)

**To see Jesus.** (*hold hand over eyes*)

**The tombstone was rolled away,** (*roll your hands over each other*)

**Rolled away, rolled away.** (*roll hands*)

**The tombstone was rolled away.** (*rolls hands*)

**It was empty.** (*open hands with palms out*)

**The angel said not to fear,** (*make arms into an "X"*)

**Not to fear, not to fear.** (*make an "X"*)

**The angel said not to fear.** (*make an "X"*)

**Jesus lives!** (*raise hands into the air*)

# Surprising News

## Action Play

**SUPPLIES**

**R**ead your preschoolers the following rhyme, having them follow along as you do the actions in parentheses while you read each line. Have kids start out squatting.

Rhyme:

**Just as the sun was rising,** *(slowly stand up)*

**Mary found something surprising.** *(raise eyebrows, and put hands on cheeks in surprise)*

**The stone was rolled away.** *(roll hands)*

**An angel had to say:** *(cup hands around mouth)*

**"You have nothing to fear,** *(point to kids)*

**Jesus isn't here."** *(shake head "no")*

Encourage kids to shout, "Jesus is alive!"

# Empty Tomb Prayer

## Prayer

**SUPPLIES**

**G**ather kids together in a circle to pray. Instead of folding hands, have kids cup their hands together, palms facing each other and fingers touching. Go around the circle, asking kids to take turns praying out loud. Have kids open their hands and pray about one reason they're thankful for Jesus.

Encourage children to use their cupped hands to show someone this week what they learned about the empty tomb and Jesus being alive.

# Jesus' Followers Share His Good News

## Matthew 28:16-20; Acts 1:6-11

## Jesus Sends the Disciples

### Bible Experience

**SUPPLIES**
Bible

**H**ave kids gather in a circle. Open your Bible to Matthew 28 or Acts 1, and show the children the words. Tell them the Bible is God's special book.

Say: **After Jesus came back to life, the disciples went to a place called Galilee to find Jesus. When they found him, they worshipped him.** Have kids worship Jesus by shouting, "We love you, Jesus!" **Some of the disciples still had a hard time believing Jesus really was alive.**

Ask:

- *Tell about a time someone told you something you didn't believe.*
- *How did you find out whether or not they were telling you the truth?*

Say: **Jesus spoke to all his friends, telling them to go into the rest of the world to tell people about Jesus and find other people who would follow him.**

Ask:

- *Tell about a time you had really good news to share.*
- *Who are some people you can tell the good news about Jesus and heaven?*

Say: **Jesus also told the disciples that the Holy Spirit would come and give them power to be witnesses for him.**

**When Jesus was done telling the disciples all these things, he started rising up into the sky.**

**Eventually Jesus disappeared into a cloud. Then two angels appeared, standing next to the disciples. They told the disciples that one day Jesus would return in just the same way—coming down from heaven through the clouds.**

Ask:

- *What does it mean to you to know that Jesus is coming back someday?*
- *How does knowing that Jesus is coming back help you today?*

Say: **Jesus wants us to tell everyone about him!**

# Watching for Jesus

## Craft

**SUPPLIES**

2 cardboard tubes per child, strips of construction paper cut as wide as the cardboard tubes are long, scissors, washable markers, yarn, tape

**S**ay: **Let's make something that helps us remember to keep looking for Jesus.**

Give each child two cardboard tubes and a strip of construction paper. Help children tape the paper tubes together side by side to make binoculars. Then show children how to cover the tubes by wrapping construction paper around them. Set out markers, and let children color their binoculars in any way they choose. Help children make a neck strap for their binoculars by taping the ends of a piece of yarn to the outer side of each of the tubes.

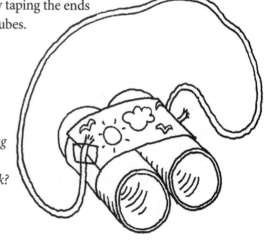

As kids work, ask the following questions.

Ask:

- *What are some things you like to watch in the sky?*
- *Why is it important to remember Jesus is coming back?*
- *What can you do to watch for Jesus coming back?*

Say: **Jesus will come back one day. We can be ready for him!**

# Follow the Follower

## Game

SUPPLIES

**S**ay: **The disciples learned to do what Jesus wanted by being with him. When the disciples went out and told people about Jesus, they had to be examples to others of what Jesus wanted them to do. Let's play a version of Follow the Leader to see what that's like.**

Separate the children into pairs. Have pairs face each other. As the leader, stand so only one partner in each pair can see you. Perform a number of actions for this partner to imitate. Then as the partner imitates your actions, the other partner should imitate those actions. After a few minutes, have partners switch places and play again. If you have an uneven number of kids, you might choose one child to be the leader.

Ask:

- *What was it like to be an example to your partner?*
- *What would make this game easier?*
- *How can you be an example to others of how Jesus wants you to live?*

Say: **Let's do what Jesus has told us to do every day.**

# Sharing About Jesus

## Snack

**SUPPLIES**

bananas cut in half with peels on (1 half per child), small paper plates, chocolate chips, craft sticks, antibacterial gel (optional)

*ALLERGY ALERT!*
See page 5

**H**ave kids clean their hands before preparing the snacks. Give each child half a banana on a paper plate. Have kids each peel their banana. Then help them insert a craft stick into the flat end of the banana. Show kids how to push the tips of the chocolate chips into the banana to make eyes and a nose.

Say: **Jesus wants us to tell other people about him.**

Using the banana people as puppets, have kids role-play talking to others about Jesus. Warn kids not to touch one another's banana people.

When kids are done, let them eat and enjoy their treats. As kids eat, ask the following questions.

Ask:

- *What was it like to tell someone about Jesus?*
- *What do you think are the most important things to tell people about Jesus?*

Say: **Think about ways you can tell your friends about Jesus!**

## Good News!

## Song

**SUPPLIES**

**S**ay: **Let's sing a song to help us tell others about Jesus.** Teach preschoolers the following words to the tune of "Jingle Bells." Sing it through several times, having children take turns filling in the blank at the end with something they know Jesus gives them—like food or family or friends.

Sing:

**I've got news—great, great news.**

**Jesus is my friend.**

**He gives me love. He gives me joy.**

**He also gives me** [name something given to you by Jesus].

# Climbing up a Mountain

## Action Play

**SUPPLIES**

**R**ead your preschoolers the following rhyme, having them follow along as you do the actions in parentheses while you read each line.

Rhyme:

**We're climbing up a mountain.** *(climb with arms and legs)*

**We'll meet with Jesus there.** *(point up)*

**We'll bow down and worship him** *(bow at the waist)*

**When we see him there.** *(shade eyes with hands)*

**When Jesus starts a-speakin',** *(cup hands around mouth)*

**He tells us we can share** *(cup hands together in front)*

**His love with those around us,** *(sweep hands out)*

**That his spirit's always near.** *(put hands on heart)*

**When Jesus finished speaking,** *(cup hands around mouth)*

**He rose up in the air.** *(jump in the air)*

**"He's coming back," is what we heard** *(cup hands to ears)*

**When his angels did appear.** *(flap arms like wings)*

# Pass It On Prayer

## Prayer

**S**ay: **Let's pray in a way that reminds us to tell others about Jesus.**

Gather kids in a circle to pray. Go around the circle, inviting kids to pray in any way they choose. They can tell Jesus they love him, ask forgiveness for something they've done wrong, or pray for a need in their life. After children have a turn to pray, have them pass a turn on to the person next to them by giving that person a hug and saying, "Jesus loves you." Start the prayer time yourself; then pass the turn on to the child on your right.

After everyone has had a turn, close the time by thanking God for the kids in your group and the time you have with them.

# God Frees Paul and Silas From Prison

## Acts 16:16-34

## Prisoners Set Free

### Bible Experience

 SUPPLIES

Bible, masking tape

**B**efore children arrive, tape off a square corner of the room large enough for everyone to sit in. This will be your prison cell.

Have kids sit in a circle with you. Open your Bible to Acts 16, and show children the words. Tell kids the Bible is God's special book.

Say: **The Bible tells about Paul and Silas, who loved Jesus so much they traveled all over to tell people about him.**

Ask:

- *Tell about some places you've traveled.*
- *What kinds of things did you do while you were there?*

Say: **Paul and Silas also helped people and healed people in Jesus' name. One day in a town called Philippi, Paul and Silas helped a little slave girl by freeing her from a bad spirit. But the slave girl's owner didn't think that was helpful, because the slave girl earned a lot of money for him. So her owner had Paul and Silas beaten and thrown into jail.** Have kids sit in the prison cell and imagine they're sitting in a prison.

Ask:

- *Tell about a time someone was mean to you.*
- *What did you do?*

Say: **Paul and Silas didn't complain or get upset because they were in prison. They actually started singing songs to Jesus and praising God. Paul and Silas remembered how important it is to praise God even when we're sad or when hard things happen to us.** Lead kids in singing a verse of "Jesus Loves Me" in praise to God.

**In the middle of the night, God sent a great big earthquake. And when that happened, the prison doors opened up and all the prisoners' chains came off.** Have kids jump up and down as if they've just been freed.

**Instead of leaving the prison, though, Paul and Silas stayed right there.** Have kids sit down again in the prison cell. **They convinced the other prisoners to stay as well. They knew that the jailer would be punished if they escaped. And because Paul and Silas stayed, they got to share the good news about Jesus with the jailer. And the jailer decided to become one of Jesus' followers, too!**

Ask:

- *Who do you know that you could tell about Jesus?*
- *What are some of the good things you could tell your friends about Jesus?*

Say: **God is always watching over us. He loves us and wants what's best for us.**

# Shackles

## Craft

**SUPPLIES**

two 3-inch wide strips of construction paper per child, crayons, 1-foot lengths of yarn, scissors, tape

**S**ay: **The guards threw Paul and Silas into a dark prison and put them in chains called shackles. Let's make some shackles to see what they were like.**

Give each child two strips of construction paper. Let kids color one side of each paper strip any way they choose. Help kids wrap one strip of construction paper—picture side out—around each wrist. Trim as necessary, and tape the ends of the paper strips together to form shackles. Leave the shackles wide enough to slide over kids' hands. Help kids attach the ends of a length of yarn to each shackle with tape.

Ask:

- *What kinds of things would be hard to do if you were wearing shackles?*
- *Why is it easier to do things when your hands are free?*

Say: **God used Paul and Silas' time in prison to help the jailer know about Jesus. Even though they weren't free, they still told people around them all about Jesus!**

# Earthquake!

## Game

**S**ay: **Let's play a game of Tag to remember that God sent an earthquake to break Paul and Silas' chains.**

Choose one child to be the Jailer (tagger). Explain to kids that when they're tagged, they must link arms with either the Jailer or the previous person who was tagged to form a chain.

After a few minutes of play, yell out "Earthquake!" When you do, everyone must stop and stomp their feet to make the rumbling noise of an earthquake. All of the kids who've been caught can break their chains and go free. But before they do, they must form a circle around the Jailer and say "God loves you." Choose another child to be the Jailer for the next round, and continue playing.

Ask:

- *What was it like to be chained together?*
- *God helped Paul and Silas by sending an earthquake. Tell about a time God helped you with a problem.*
- *The jailer wanted to know about God because Paul and Silas stayed in prison even though they could have escaped. What can we do to help other people learn about Jesus?*

Say: **God wants to show his power in your life, too!**

# Cupcake Prisons

## Snack

### SUPPLIES

1 frosted cupcake (homemade or store bought) per child, thin pretzel sticks, graham cracker squares, 2 gummy bears per child, paper plates, antibacterial gel (optional)

ALLERGY ALERT!
See page 5

**H**ave kids clean their hands before preparing their snacks. Give each child a frosted cupcake and a handful of pretzels on a paper plate. Help kids push pretzel sticks into the tops of their cupcakes around the outer edge to look like prison bars. Let kids each place two gummy bears in the middle of their cupcakes to represent Paul and Silas; then have kids place a graham cracker square on top of the pretzels for a roof.

Ask:

- *The prison cell Paul and Silas were in was pretty scary. Tell about a time you felt scared.*
- *What does God do to help you when you're scared?*
- *Paul and Silas sang songs of praise to God when they were in prison. What songs help remind you that God is always with you?*

If time allows, sing some of the songs mentioned by kids as they enjoy their snacks.

# Singin' in Chains

## Song

### SUPPLIES

**A**sk the kids to cross their arms and legs and pretend that they are in chains. For added effect, dim or turn off the lights.

Say: **Paul and Silas had a lot of reason to complain or feel bad. But instead they sang songs to God. Let's sing a song to Jesus while we're in our pretend chains! Singing songs to Jesus can help us feel joy even when times get tough.**

Sing a simple praise song with the kids. Then let them break their pretend chains.

Ask:

- *What are some of your favorite church songs?*
- *Name some other times and places we can sing songs to Jesus like Paul and Silas did.*

Say: **Singing songs to Jesus can help us when we're having a hard time. He loves to hear from us.**

# Set Free

## Action Play

SUPPLIES

**R**ead preschoolers the following rhyme about God freeing Paul and Silas from prison, having them follow along as you do the actions in parentheses while you read each line.

Rhyme:

**Once there was a man named Paul** *(stand up tall)*

**And his friend named Silas.** *(link arms with a neighbor)*

**When they were on their way to pray,** *(make praying hands)*

**A slave girl followed them each day.** *(walk in place)*

**Her owners locked the friends in prison** *(hold fists on either side of face like holding prison bars)*

**And fastened their feet in chains.** *(touch feet)*

**But the prisoners prayed and sang all night** *(make praying hands)*

**Until they heard a loud bang!** *(cover ears with hands)*

**The earth shook up and down.** *(move hands up and down in front)*

**The chains on their feet fell off.** *(touch feet; then quickly raise hands above head)*

**The prison doors opened wide.** *(place hands on chest; then sweep hands out)*

**But Paul and Silas stayed inside.** *(point down)*

**The jailer didn't know what to think.** *(scratch head)*

**It was dark; he couldn't see.** *(cover eyes with hands)*

**But once he went and got a light,** *(take hands away from eyes like playing peekaboo)*

**Praise God! He was saved that night!** *(put arms above head and wiggle hands)*

# Prayer Helpers

## Prayer

**H**ave kids sit in a circle with you for prayer.

Say: **God helped Paul and Silas by sending an earthquake. Paul and Silas helped the jailer by not escaping and by telling him about Jesus. The jailer helped Paul and Silas by feeding them and caring for their wounds. Let's pray prayers of help for one another.**

Go around the circle, inviting kids to take turns praying for one another. Start the prayer off yourself, praying for the child on your left. Keep it simple, as kids will be looking to you for examples. Then have children continue praying around the circle, praying for the child on their left. They can thank God for the other person, pray that person would feel God's love, or pray for a specific need in that child's life.

Close the time with a prayer of thanks for the way God helps us every day.

# God Saves Paul From a Shipwreck

## Acts 27:13-44

## A Scary Ride

### Bible Experience

**SUPPLIES**

Bible, empty 2-liter bottle with a cap, water, dish soap, pencil that will float or a piece of cork

**TIP**

For extra impact, find a small plastic boat that's small enough to fit inside the bottle and floats.

**B**efore children arrive, fill a clean 2-liter bottle about two-thirds full of water and a few drops of dish soap. Put a pencil that will float (or a piece of cork) inside the bottle to simulate a boat. Place the cap securely on the bottle.

Have kids sit in a circle with you. Open your Bible to Acts 27, and show children the words. Tell them the Bible is God's special book.

Say: **The Bible tells about a time Paul took a really exciting—and scary—trip in the water.**

Ask:

- *What's the most exciting trip you've ever taken?*

Say: **Paul was being taken to prison by boat. While Paul and the sailors were on the way, a great storm blew up and tossed the boat around.** Pass around the bottle with the pencil or cork in it, letting kids take turns shaking the bottle and watching it rise to the top. As kids look at and shake the bottle, continue telling what happened to Paul.

The storm lasted two weeks. The wind blew so hard the sailors couldn't steer the boat. They also had to tie ropes around the boat to keep it from breaking apart. Then everyone started throwing things overboard to make the ship lighter.

Because of the storm, the people couldn't see the sun or the stars. They thought they were lost.

Ask:

- *Tell about a time you got lost.*
- *What was it like for you when you were lost?*

Say: **One night during the storm, an angel appeared to Paul and told him God said no one would get hurt in the storm—even though the ship would be ruined. God wanted Paul to be safe. So God promised everyone would land safely on an island.**

**Paul believed what the angel told him. He stood up on the ship and told everyone else what the angel had said to encourage them.**

Ask:

- *Tell about a time someone encouraged you.*
- *How did that person's encouragement help you?*

Say: **At the end of two weeks the sailors started to realize they were getting close to land. They were excited to finally get to land. But they were also afraid they wouldn't be able to see the land since it was so dark, and they worried the ship would crash. They wished it would be light out so they could see better.** Help kids form pairs and take turns leading each other around the center of the room with their eyes closed.

Ask:

- *What was it like walking around with your eyes closed?*
- *Why can it be scary to be in the dark?*

Say: **Everyone on the boat was so scared they couldn't eat. But Paul encouraged them to eat so they could stay strong.** Have kids pretend to eat and drink as you continue.

**When it finally got to be light again, everyone saw they were close to an island with a beach. The sailors tried to steer the boat toward the beach. But just under the water where they couldn't see it was hard ground. The boat got stuck. Then the boat started to break apart, and everyone fell into the water. The people who were able to swam to the beach. The rest of the people floated to the beach by holding onto things like broken pieces of wood.** Have kids pretend to either swim or float in the water.

Ask:

- *Tell about a time you were in the water.*
- *What was it like for you to be in the water?*

Say: **For the people on the boat with Paul, it was a scary. But everyone was safe, just as God promised.**

# Planter-Box Boats

## Craft

**B**efore kids arrive, cut off the top 3 to 4 inches and bottom 3 to 4 inches of each box for use as boat planters. Cut triangles from construction paper for sails.

Say: **God kept Paul and everyone with him on the boat safe from the storm. Let's make something to remind us God can protect us, too.**

Give each child a top or bottom box section. Help kids use masking tape to completely cover the outside of their box sections to make boats. Set out markers and stickers, and let kids decorate the outside of their boats however they choose. Help kids fill their boats with 2 to 3 inches of potting soil, and let them push a few seeds into the soil.

Give each child two construction paper triangles and a craft stick. Have kids tape the two paper triangles to the craft stick to make a sail. Then let kids put their sails into their boats by pushing the end the craft stick into the soil.

Ask:

- *The ship Paul was on carried people and food. What other things do ships carry?*

Say: **Just as God kept Paul safe, the soil in our cardboard boats will keep the seeds safe until they can grow into beautiful flowers.**

Ask:

- *What are some things God wants us to do?*
- *What ways does God protect us?*

Remind kids to water their seeds and place their planter-box boats in sunlight so the flowers will grow.

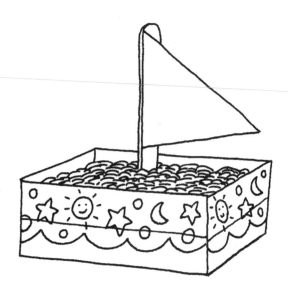

# Stand Your Ground

## Game

**S**ay: **Let's play a little game called Stand Your Ground. One person will try to stand here and not move while the rest of us try to get that person to move. We can't touch anyone or throw anything. We can only make noises and move our bodies.**

Have kids take turns trying to stand still while others distract them.

Ask:

- *Explain whether it was easy or hard for you to stand still.*
- *Pretend you're on Paul's ship during the storm at sea, right before the shipwreck. What scary things might you see and hear that make you want to move around?*
- *How did you stand still even when people were yelling and moving all around you?*

Say: **Some of us stood still because we knew no matter how loud or crazy others were, nothing would hurt us. Imagine standing still even if the room were shaking. Paul stood still and was brave even when his ship was destroyed because he believed God when God said he'd be safe.**

# S.S. Orange

## Snack

**H**ave kids clean their hands before preparing the snack.

Say: **Let's make a snack to remember how God comforted Paul on his stormy boat ride.**

Give each child an orange half and a cheese triangle on a paper plate. Help kids push one end of a toothpick into their cheese triangle and the other end into their orange to make a sailboat.

Ask:

- *Tell about a time you rode on a boat.*
- *Paul's boat ride was scary. When have you been scared?*
- *God sent an angel to tell Paul not to be afraid. What are some ways God comforts you when you're afraid?*

# Paul Was Riding in a Boat

## Song

SUPPLIES
none

**S**ay: **Let's sing a song to help us remember that God kept Paul safe in the storm.**
Teach kids the following words and motions to the tune of "If You're Happy and
You Know It."

Sing:

**One day Paul was riding in a boat,** *(make waves with hands)*

**When a storm came and tossed him all about.** *(lean side to side)*

**His boat crashed on an island,** *(clap hands to sound like a crash)*

**But God was still beside him.** *(stand tall)*

**Paul made it safe and "Praise God!" was his shout.** *(raise hands above head)*

# Dangerous Storm, Safe Passage

## Action Play

SUPPLIES
none

**R**ead children the following rhyme about Paul's shipwreck, encouraging them
to follow along as you do the actions in parentheses while you read each line. Have
kids begin by sitting.

Rhyme:

**Paul took a trip on a boat.** *(row a boat)*

**And then, while they were afloat,** *(hold arms out to the side; then bounce them up
and down as if floating)*

**A storm got its spark** *(raise fists above head, then open hands quickly)*

**And it got really dark.** *(place hands on head and raise shoulders as if scared)*

**It was like being on Noah's ark.** *(cup hands like a boat and make it float)*

**The wind tossed the boat side to side.** *(lean side to side)*

**The sailors just wanted to hide.** *(cover face with hands)*

**The people were scared,** *(place fists on chest and hunch shoulders)*

**So Paul stood and shared** *(stand up tall)*

**That an angel said all would be spared.** *(stand tall and cup hands to mouth)*

**The boat crashed onto an island** *(clap hands to make a crashing sound)*

**After two long weeks in the storm.** *(hold up two fingers)*

**The boat was wrecked,** *(cup hands together like a boat; then turn hands down)*

**But when Paul checked,** *(shade eyes with hands)*

**Every person God did protect.** *(shout "Hooray!" and jump up and down)*

# God Is Watching Over Me
## Prayer

**SUPPLIES**

**H**ave children sit in a circle with you.

Say: **God watched over Paul and everyone on the boat when they were in the storm. Let's pray and remember that God watches over us, too.**

Teach preschoolers the following words and actions.

Pray:

**God** *(point up)*

**Is watching** *(point to eyes)*

**Over** *(touch hands together over head in an arch)*

**Me.** *(point both thumbs toward chest)*

Go around the circle, giving each child a turn to pray. Children can thank God for watching over them, ask God to help them with something, tell God they love him, or anything else they choose. After each child prays, have everyone repeat the words and actions above before moving on to the next child.

Close the time by praying yourself, thanking God for watching over everyone in the group.

# Indexes

## Category

## Index

# Crafts

# Games

# Prayers

# Songs

## Snacks

# Scripture

## Index

THE **GIANT** BOOK OF PRESCHOOL IDEAS FOR CHILDREN'S MINISTRY

# Topic
## Index